The Boomerpreneur Revolution

How Baby Boomers Are Turning Their Knowledge Into Profits

BY RICHARD GREHALVA

Published by: P2P People to People Communications Media

Sales/Marketing

ISBN: 978-0-9763818-2-2
Digital: www.richardgrehalva.com

Over 50 Entrepreneurs - Free Video eCourse with Tips to Turn your Knowledge into Profits

Your knowledge is needed, wanted and valuable!

ARE YOU READY TO JOIN:

THE

BOOMERPRENEUR

REVOLUTION?

This FREE program contains 10 videos to help you answer the question about your business "Where Do I Start?" and What Do I Need to Succeed?

YOU'LL DISCOVER:

- What questions to ask yourself before you start your business
- The steps to write and publish your eBook to establish you as an expert
- How to create a consulting packages to sell online
- My 5 best tips on starting your business and the mindset to have to succeed. Recorded live at Mike Koeing's AEEM February 2013 Live Event in San Diego, CA

And much more!

Get instant access, right now!

GET THE

FREE

VIDEOS NOW!

Text your name and email address to (858) 433-4389

WITH A SHORT CODE

Text the keyword boomer to 58885 add your name and email address to get instant access

SCAN THIS QR CODE

OR VISIT THIS WEB PAGE

www.Over50Entreprenurs.com

Dedication

This book is dedicated to Wende, my wife of over 30 years. She has stuck it out with me, and I'm grateful for her support and love. I look forward to the next 30 years, as we enter into retirement on our terms.

This book is also dedicated to the all the Baby Boomers who have knowledge to share. The gifts you were given along the road of life are not yours to keep. You must give them away.

Table of Contents

Introduction

Welcome to The "Boomerpreneur Revolution"

"The Times Are A-Changin" -Bob Dylan

If you remember when Bob Dylan's song was first played over the radio, then you are a child of the 60s. Our generation began to question "what was" and "what it could be," and this has not changed as we have gotten older. "The times are a-changin"...*again!* We are now on the edge of an entrepreneurship boom led by the baby boomer generation.

What is it? I call it the *"Boomerpreneur Revolution"* What do we have that is valuable in this revolution? Knowledge and Experience! How valuable is our knowledge? *11 billion dollars!*

According to research director, John LaRosa: *"It appears that small, entrepreneurial companies often fare better in this market than large corporations. We expect them to fill voids in the market. Lackluster performance by such companies as Nightingale-Conant, and more recently, OWN, show that many don't yet understand the self-improvement consumer, or don't embrace new technology."*

A recent report was published by Marketdata Enterprises, Inc. on the U.S. Market for Self Improvement Products and Services. The study looks at the market from 2003-2014, through the following areas:

- Infomercials
- Holistic Institutes
- Books & Audiobooks
- Motivational Speakers
- Websites
- Seminars
- Personal Coaching
- Online education
- Weight Loss
- Stress Management Programs

Public Seminars

Attendance at live events and small training seminars (a $400-500 million market) has taken a major hit, due to increased travel costs. *Webinars* (seminars given online) have filled the void and have become more popular due to lower cost and 24/7 availability.

Shift to Online Programs - Less Overhead, More Profits

Self-improvement services are now being delivered via audio, video and over the Internet. Coaching is performed by phone. Motivational speakers that are tired of the road can hold live teleseminars or webinars. This broadens their market to consumers who don't want to spend the money on travel and lodging.

Gurus can also provide online courses for home study. Several large self-help websites exist, such as Beliefnet.com and Self-growth.com.

Books

Flat is the new up. There were no blockbusters for the past two years, as the market was flooded with political content. Marketdata estimates that self-improvement book sales were worth $776 million in 2011.

Audiobooks Market

The APA says that 24+ million Americans now listen to audiobooks. Of this total, self-improvement titles account for $455 million—or about 17% of all audiobook sales.

There is a notable lack of speakers and content serving the Generation X or Y younger consumer. This is a huge untapped market, as most companies still pursue Baby Boomers.

Knowledge is Profitable

Our "knowledge" as you can see, is very valuable. There is no shortage of what people will buy to get what you know. You can fill the gap between what is missing and what they want to improve on in their personal and professional effectiveness and success.

We have the information, knowledge and wisdom to perform all kinds of activities from improving relationships, making more money, career performance and advancement, hobbies, crafts—the list goes on. If you can talk about whatever it is you are passionate about, and teach it, then you can develop and sell information products.

You can create audios, videos, seminars, books and more with what you know. Do not cut yourself short. People want what you know, so why not share it and make money doing what you enjoy in your retirement years?

My goal with this book is to teach you... how.

Why Now?

Did you know that the next business to be launched will not be from a 20-something, but more than likely it will be someone over the age of 55? According to the research done by the Kauffman Foundation: *"In every single year from 1996 to 2007, Americans between the ages of 55 and 64 had a higher rate of entrepreneurial activity than those aged 20-34."*

The Bureau of Labor Statistics data shows self-employment as an even more extreme pattern. The rate of self-employment is higher among people in their 60s than even those in their 50s, let alone those in their 20s or 30s. In fact, the bureau's surveys of American workers reveal that people aged 65 to 69 are self-employed heads of corporations at four times the rate of people aged 25 to 34.

The Small Business Administration reports in its recently released publication *Small Business Economy* that, from 2000 to 2011:

- Self-employment for people under 25 dropped 9 percent.
- For people aged 25 to 34, it fell 8 percent.
- For people between 35 and 44, it declined 24 percent.

Here is the big news!

- Self-employment for people aged 55 to 64 rose 54 percent!
- It increased 36 percent for those over 65.

Okay, you get the picture now. More than ever, baby boomers are becoming entrepreneurs... *Boomerpreneurs.*

I bet you did not know that 401ks were developed to supplement our social security and pensions. Now we are looking to our 401ks to be the primary source of income with social security as a supplement, and pension plans, who has that? Or how about saving your money and living off the interest from your money market account? No, not with today's interest rates.

We need a way to not be dependent on what the government or stock market does, and this can be done by creating a business. This is a way of producing our own supplemental income in our retirement.

Why Me?

Many people over 55 want the opportunity to create a business that meets their unique needs, interests, and desires to make a difference.

According to an AARP survey conducted in 2011, almost 80% of people 55 and over want to continue working, more than half in part-time work; the motivation:

- they need or want additional income
- they have a desire to continue in productive activities
- they recognized they may be living for 30 more years or longer

People over 55 have many years of experience, expertise, seasoned judgment, and proven performance to support creating a new business.

People over 55 have developed excellent contacts in the business world that can help their new-business venture.

People over 55 have accumulated enough money to support a new business.

People over 55 want productive activities like having their own business. And those that do live longer, enjoy better health, and report greater satisfaction with life compared to those who don't.

Today, the internet has been the single biggest game changer. The barriers to entry are minimal. You can set up a blog for free, you can post videos on YouTube for free, you can publish a Kindle ebook for free and you can even build a website for free.

To succeed it takes good planning, a product or service that people want and will pay for, the willingness to put in the effort, and the hours to make your business work. Once it is launched and people begin to buy your product or service, it is incredibly gratifying.

Do You Have a Boomerpreneur Mindset?

What should you do before launching into building your own business? First, you need to have a different mindset. I have 9 questions for you to ask yourself, so get out a piece of paper and answer each question honestly to find out if you have the mindset to begin your second-half career as a Boomerpreneur.

1. **What problem can you clearly describe and solve in a few sentences?** This is a vital first step in understanding what you can deliver to your prospective market.

2. **Are you okay with building a low-cost home office business?** If you have been a professional in a corporation who is used to the office setup with all the trimmings, and you want to spend their kind of money duplicating this environment, you will be wasting your money. Get over it.

3. **How comfortable are you with making decisions?** You will no longer have others to direct you, it is all up to you and being decisive is the key. Analysis paralysis can contribute to failure.

4. **How good are your contacts?** Write down your prospective clients by creating a persona. Then, who do you

know needs your service or product, or can introduce you to someone who does? How much income do you need? Don't be taken in by the hype of becoming an instant, overnight-millionaire. Figure out how much you require to live the lifestyle you want. It may be anywhere from $3 to $5000. The aim is to be clear on your goal.

5. **Are you willing to learn?** Let's face it, the clock is ticking and you are not going to have all the skills to launch your business. You will need to learn or outsource certain tasks.

6. **Are you tech savvy?** You need to understand auto-responders, SEO, keywords, building effective PowerPoint presentations, and more. This means being updated with technology. If you don't have these skills, you will need to learn quickly or again, outsource the functions.

7. **Are you committed to the time it will take to launch your business?** It is very possible to make $50,000 to $100,000 a year income by only working two to three days a week. The reality is, this will not happen for the first two years.

8. **How is your support group?** Do you have a mentor and friends that can help and support you? You must get support from your family and especially your spouse; be transparent with them and involve them.

9. **Are you ready?** People need information to take action. Most of them get the information but don't take action... don't be one of them.

Whatever reasons you have behind your decision to start working from home, it's a given that you want to be successful, and the good news? Thousands of people run successful businesses from home, with more joining the Boomerpreneur ranks every day. They may not make headlines as the latest overnight millionaire successes, but they earn a comfortable living and find satisfaction in their work, while spending more time with their families and less time behind a corporate desk.

Why You Should Go Online

From what point should you start your business? Well, there are only three choices:

1. Build a business from scratch
2. Buy an existing business
3. Buy a franchise

Each one has its pros and cons, but the one I will focus on is building your own business from scratch, for the least amount of money and for the quickest return.

When I speak to people I coach, or the businesses I consult with, I ask them this question: *"Why are you the best at what you do?"* The number one answer is - "I don't know I just do it." They learned the proper way to do something, and then through trial and error, they discovered a short cut that is highly effective.

Have you accomplished the same thing in your career or life?

What is it that you know? What is the knowledge that you possess that's going to make a difference in the lives of others?

Is it going to help them advance in their career?
Is it going to allow them to be healthier?
Is it going to help them in their investments?
Is it going to help them improve their business performance?
Is it going to help improve their relationships?
Is it something that will help them with a hobby, to make it more enjoyable?

Just think of what you do well and are passionate for. Begin to list the exact sequence of what you do, and don't judge it or try to change it. This will become the foundation of building processes, products and services later on.

To help you to discover what this is, I have 3 questions for you to answer.

1. What is it that you want to offer?
2. What are the skills that you have to bring it to offer?
3. Why does the world need it?

Now once you answer those three questions, then you have the formulation of what you will need in starting your own business.

A business owner, a Boomerpreneur – like you – has a different goal, perspective, and motivation compared to a 20, 30 or 40 year old. You want to create a business that will provide you with the kind of life you deserve, the financial freedom and the flexibility to enjoy semi-retirement. You want to create a business on your terms that meets your expectations not those of someone else.

A business owner fills several roles: he or she is the CEO, the manager, the technical manager, the accountant, the writer. Starting an online business or businesses that you can promote with relative ease is the reason why building a business online is inexpensive, and the barriers to entry are minimal.

When people are in need of something in today's world, ninety-percent of them do not go to the Yellow Pages. The first thing they do is they search online. You might be reading this book after you decided to build a business and went online to search for information that would help you, am I right?

Creating the Life You Deserve In Retirement

The internet has made it possible for you to share your passions, skills and knowledge with the world. It has made it possible to create the life you want, which means:

- Creating supplemental retirement income
- Passing your valuable knowledge and skills on to people who need and want it
- Communicating and partnering with like minded individuals
- Spending time on your passions
- Learning from and helping others
- Enjoying your life

The internet has made it possible for you to create a business which supports your goals, whatever they may be. An internet business helps create the life you want in retirement, by providing additional income for vacations, travel or perhaps just to afford those extra luxuries.

So how do you go from wanting to start your business to actually having the life you desire? The question becomes:

What Does it Take to be a Boomerpreneur?

Here are six key areas to explore before you get started.

1. **Are you ready to run all of the aspects of your business?** You know it's going to be totally up to you. There isn't going to be someone there, there is no boss telling you what to do. You're going to have to develop the project and organize your time to follow through on the details. Is this something you're willing to do?

2. **Do have planning skills?** Research shows that many business fail for not having enough cash, but did you know another major reason is poor planning?

3. **How will your business have an impact on your family?** The first few years of a business start-up is tough on you and your family. This is the time to have a meeting with your spouse to get buy-in and support. The next is to have the meeting with your family to get their support. Be transparent. Share all the information you have because your spouse is your partner in life and both of you will share the rewards of your business.

4. **You report to yourself.** This is really the cool part. It's all up to you and you can take advantage of the opportunity when you see it. Here is the warning: do not fall into the trap of the next cool thing. It is very easy to do this and when that happens, you will never finish anything. Make sure you have the discipline to finish one project, and then go on to the next.

5. **What does it take to run a successful business?** Use the answers from these questions and you will be successful. Remember, you have the years of wise experience on your side.

6. **There is no easy button.** Please do not believe the hype that you find on the internet; all the push button success of

becoming a millionaire overnight, having a Ferrari in your driveway, living in a mansion and traveling around the world... and all you need to do is work one hour a day, *really?* When you build your online business, like anything else it's going to take time, so you need to be realistic in your income goals and expectations. Hard work, determination, believing in what you do, using marketing and having a good plan is what it takes, but you already know that.

The Sherpa Guide

Sherpa guides lead their clients on the safest path to take. For those who have decided to take on their goal of scaling Mt. Everest, the Sherpa guide shows them the steps to take, where the safe footing is, and which areas are unsafe. The final ascent is no longer up to the Sherpa guide. It is up to their client to scale the summit to the top on their own. This is what this book is designed to help you achieve. It's dedicated to show you where to step, and just like the Sherpa, the final climb to the summit is up to you.

The mountain peak each person chooses as his or her own destination, is his or her own path. A person who wants a 4 hour work week is going to have a much different path than a person who seeks a business where he or she is focused on his or her passion, and his or her definition of success could be 40 hours a week. Neither path is wrong if it follows your definition of success and what you want for your life – your vision.

The challenge is to create a plan to get you there; there are many steps along the way. The first and most important step is defining what success means to you. If you haven't written down what success means to you, take a moment and write it down. Writing it down is helpful because it helps you stay on track. It's easy to get lost in the day to day when building a business. Defining success to yourself helps you stay focused and make decisions based on the bigger picture. So go ahead, set everything aside for a moment, grab a piece of paper and write down what success looks like to you. If you're not a writer and would rather verbalize it, grab a tape recorder, close your eyes and visualize success. Describe what you see out loud. You can refer to the recording or have someone transcribe it for you to refer to later.

Despite the idea that an online business is doomed before you even start, there are many successful Boomerpreneurs who know better. The Internet makes it possible to reach people all over the world. This means having an online business can find a niche and create a successful company that would have been impossible to maintain through traditional methods. There are billions of people online today. You only have to reach a fraction of a percent of them to become a successful Internet marketer. If you reach the right audience, you can create a profitable online business, and enjoy all the benefits of working from home.

This book will show you how.

Why do so many people fail to make money online even though they did everything they were supposed to? Why are two people who are in the same business niche, using the same marketing tools available, and one fails where the other does not?

Why does someone who has been building his or her business for years suddenly get passed by a 'newcomer' out of nowhere? Why are some people who seem very successful on the outside, not satisfied or happy on the inside?

These questions and more I've asked myself over and over again, and these are probably questions you have also asked yourself at some point in your life. I have grown tired of seeing my friends and fellow baby boomers and potential Boomerpreneurs give up on their dreams because they simply did not know where to start, or they were thinking that they couldn't start a business.

As I said, what baby boomers have that is valuable is *knowledge.* I have put what works, and what you need to know to build your information products, into 5 steps that will take what you know, monetize it, and successfully launch your business. I call them *'The 5 Knowledge Business Activators."*

Here is quick summary of the activators:

Knowledge Activator number 1: *"Know Yourself."* Your success begins and ends with you. You will discover your specific motivation triggers to accelerate your performance on a daily basis.

Knowledge Activator number 2: *"Know your Message."* We establish your positioning strategy in your market niche.

Knowledge Activator number 3: *"Know your Market."* We will be creating your product blueprint by applying the formula — problem plus result equals a solution.

Knowledge Activator number 4: *"Know your Business."* Developing your business model with what you will offer that is unique and valuable, instead of being not unique and not valuable.

Knowledge Activator number 5: *"Know your Movement."* Creating your Magnetic Marking Movement Strategy. We will position you as an expert with your online visibility strategy including videos, eBooks, webinars and more. You will become the trusted source in your market niche.

How to Use This Book For the Maximum Benefit

I would like to invite you to get a success journal. You can use a ledger, a regular journal book, or a pad of paper. The important thing is you have a place to write your notes and ideas. It will also be where you will write down your answers to the exercises in this book.

Have you ever gone to the grocery store to pick up a few items and when you get there you have forgotten what was on the list? Have you noticed that when you do write down your list and then you get to the grocery store, you do not even need to pull out the list, because you remember each item?

There is a reason for that power inside your brain. What I want you to know is that it is important for you to write things down in your success journal. It will help you with your recall. This is a very productive habit to learn and will serve you well.

It is important to follow what I tell you in sequence. The reason why people fail is because they want it now and they rush. Remember this: *"You have to learn to crawl before you walk, and you need to learn to walk before you run."*

This book is not a crystal ball with all the answers. It is a guide to help you create your personal path to creating and launching your business.

Let's get started!

Chapter 1
I Don't Know Where to Start

So you are ready to get going, but you have an important question: *"Where do I start?"* I was once at the same place you are now.

I had been encouraged by my friends, business associates, and family to start a business. They told me I had great insights when I spoke about business and life strategies. I was ready to take the leap, but how?

When I was 39, I had my first website built and it cost me over $6000. In those days, that was a bargain, and a far cry from where it is today, where you can easily build a website for free. I also had to have someone write the copy; I figured they would just write some great stuff. Turns out I needed to give her a bunch of details, like what products did I have, what was my unique proposition, and then I was thinking I needed to do a lot of work. I wanted to be hired to speak more, so I just wanted to put out my shingle and have it say "expert for rent."

Those were the days of just getting your brochure and creating a website. Remember it was not until 1995 did we get to hear "You've Got Mail" if you had AOL dial-up internet access. If I am dating myself here and you don't know what I'm talking about, then you are not a baby boomer.

I figured out I needed to have some products on the site, so I was going to need to have some cassette tape programs to sell... yes, I said cassette tapes. I needed to buy a tape recorder, tape duplicator, blank tapes and cases. It cost me more than I ever got back in sales.

Next, I decided I needed to have a book. The reason I wanted it is because it was difficult to get booked as a speaker without one — but — I had one simple question: *how do I do that?*

I researched and found out you need an agent. Okay, no sweat, I'd get one. Here is what agents want: "Published Authors." This was frustrating, because the advice was to just keep writing letters to agents. Yes writing, not emails, but snail mail letters. I found out that even if I got lucky and I got an agent who had an editor interested in my work, and they decided to publish it, it would still be 18 months later.

No problem, I could wait because I had visions of going out on my book tour that my publisher would set up. But no — that is now how it works. I'm not a famous author so I would need to pay all of the marketing myself. My payoff might be a 10% royalty of the discounted price. Yes, folks, book publishing is a very interesting business.

I decided to go the self-publishing route. If I was going to have to do all of this myself, why not keep all the profit? I went to seminars to learn how it was done. I had many ideas of what my book would be about, but I had no real plan.

My first time out starting a business was a failure. No surprise, since I really did not have a game plan. I did not have a system to build my online business.

The funny thing was I was working full time at the time, I was a Vice President/General Manger at Computer Sciences Corporation, a Fortune 500 company. I was involved in developing strategy and tactic plans, budgets, marketing, sales, customer relations, project management and more, but when it came to my online business I was not really applying these skills. I was treating it more as a hobby than really treating it as a business. I'm not the type who gives up easily, so I decided I needed to change my approach. I had a series of turning points over the following years that I want to share with you.

The Covey Principle

I created an event years ago when I was working at Computer Sciences Corporation. I called it "The Pebble Beach Initiative." It was held at the Inn at Spanish Bay in Monterey, California. A highlight of the event was a round of golf at the famous Pebble Beach Golf Course. The event was targeted to the "C" suite in our industry in the mid 90s. I would bring in a variety of speakers on industry issues as well as self-improvement topics.

I wanted to get Stephen Covey to speak because his book, *The 7 Habits of Highly Effective People* (c. 1989), was the top business title in 1993, but his calendar was booked so his Vice President of Consulting came to speak instead. We spent some time talking about Stephen, his background and his model. You see, I wanted to do what he was doing. I thought I could do it part time, and then go into it fully when I retired. My first attempt failed but I had not given up on my dream.

My passion, deep inside me, was that I wanted to be able to make a difference like he was; writing books, speaking, leading workshops. My question was, how did he do this? What was his model? I thought if I could figure that out then I could duplicate it. Here is what I discovered. I call it *"The Covey Principle:"*

Covey was a Harvard MBA degree holder and had spent most of his career at Brigham Young University, where he was professor of organizational behavior and business management. He was also a very devoted and spiritual man. He left BYU and started his business in 1985, as his second career, in his late 50s.

Principle number 1 - Starting a second career in your 50s can be done and be done successfully.

The Key: Believe in yourself and take the risk.

Covey said "The seven principles in the 7 Habits are not original thoughts" - he does not claim to have originated the ideas but simply to have found a framework and a language for articulating the timeless principles into the seven habits.

Principle number 2 - Take your knowledge, your passion and turn it into a format that can be used and applied to better someone's career, health, relationship, finances, or life purpose-wise.

The Key: Create a framework and turn it into a system.

I discovered following the Covey Principle in 1989, four years after he started his business and his book was published. I had the first two principles with the two keys, the foundation of the Covey Principle. Next was uncovering the business model of products and services that followed.

Principle number 3 - Write a book on your system and promote it.

Principle number 4 - Have a product to that you can sell that works with your book. In Covey's case, he had the *7 Habits Daily Planner.*

Principle number 5 - Develop a keynote speech based on your book and other related topics.

Principle number 6 - Develop a workshop that is both public, and can be customized for a client.

Principle number 7 - Develop audio and video programs.

Principle number 8 - Develop consulting and coaching programs.

Principle number 9 - Develop a certification program to allow others to use your material.

Principe number 10 - Create an online community and promote your material with blogs, forums, podcasts, videos.

Principle number 11 - Write another book! Covey wrote and published *Principle Centered Leadership* and followed the same principles.

Brilliant! It made sense, but I wanted to look at a few other successful people I admired to validate what I discovered in The Covey Principles. Brian Tracy was one of them. How did I know about him? From his books. Did you know he started his second career after the real estate company where he was COO was acquired? I looked at what he was doing and he followed the same principles. How about Tony Robbins? How did I find out about him? Yes, it was also through his books, and he followed the same principles.

I was looking for the pattern in what they all had done so I could build my own predictable and repeatable business model. Okay I got it! I then had a good idea of what I needed to do, but then came my second turning point.

When the Student is Ready, the Teacher will Appear

I remember as if it was yesterday. I was in a meeting, looking out the window, thinking I had made it. I was finally promoted to Vice President in a company with over 60,000 employees and there were only 140 of them who had the title of Vice President or above. It was a goal that I had focused on for many years, and I was pleased that I had accomplished it.

Then it hit me like a ton of bricks. I heard this question *"What's next?"*

During the next 20 years people were put in front of me at specific times to teach me a specific lesson. There were events that occurred along the way to bring a new understanding of what my path was to be. All of this was to answer the question of "What's next?"

I was fortunate to work with some mentors who taught me peak performance techniques and processes, not just in business but also in understanding what motivates people to excellence in life and business.

I also was looking and working on the inside of me, to understand what got in my way to living my purpose. I lead for over 20 years, deep and intense transformational workshops to pass on what I had learned as a certified leader with the ManKind Project. This is a non-profit organization that helps men to become better fathers, husbands, partners, uncles, and brothers by understanding what works and what does not work in their lives. I became a certified leader in the project and have led retreats all over North America and the UK.

Dr. Ron Hering was the founder of Perk Performance Consulting, and he became a mentor and a very close friend. He was the co-founder of the ManKind Project and developed a program called Accelerated Behavior Change, where I became a certified trainer. Ron taught me unbelievable processes and techniques to use with men and women to unleash and live their potential.

My father, Greywolf, was an elder and teacher. He was also called a spiritual advisor by some, while others, those who knew him, called him a medicine man. He has passed, but I was given his medicine bundle to carry on his teaching. I also had an adopted grandfather, Selo Black Crow, who taught me much about life, spirit and ceremonies. I have adopted this ancient wisdom into modern times with my programs, coaching and workshops. When I re-launched my business, this time at 50, I was ready. In the Native American community, it is not until you reach the age of 50 or 55 do you become an elder. It is because you have enough years on the planet, and you may have picked up some wisdom along the way. I was ready.

I knew that I wanted to help people in learning both business and life skills, in getting the success they were after. My own discovery was that the two must be in balance to live a fulfilling life.

Fast forward to today. Using the Covey Principle as my model, I have written and published my own books. I have a successful career as an author, speaker, consultant and coach. I have a registered trademarked sales system. My book is even a required textbook in a graduate school of management. I have multiple websites and an online information product business.

The Birth of The Grey Hair Entrepreneur

A few years ago, a friend called and wanted to meet. He is 55, a sales professional, married, with two grown children. He shared with me that his passion is executive coaching.

He wanted to figure out what he would do in retirement. Like many of us, he wanted to start a second career, and wanted my advice. He said: "I don't know where to start?" I asked what questions he had, and he began firing them off.

- Do I need a book?
- How did you get a book written?
- Do I need an agent before I write my book?
- Do I need a business plan first?
- What software did you use to build your website?
- How do you build online products?
- How do you do your videos?
- How did you write your articles?
- Is all this social stuff important?
- What do I need to know?

Then he asked me the real question: "Will you help me?"

It was not long before other baby boomers were coming to me asking the same thing. Then it came to me: the answer to the question I had asked myself 20 years earlier — "What's next?" — and "The Grey Hair Entrepreneur" was born.

I decided that I would help baby boomers to become Boomerpreneurs by turning their knowledge into profits, even if they did not know where to start, or have a business and wanted to stop trading hours for dollars. I started to search for programs that targeted baby boomers in the steps to become entrepreneurs. I found some, but not many. What I did find was plenty of websites for entrepreneurs which had for example, Internet gurus with photos of themselves posing with their Ferraris in the driveway of their mansions, with copies of the payoffs to show you how to make 6 and 7 figures overnight working only a few hours a week.

Younger people might buy the hype. They do not realize this does not happen overnight. You and I know different because *"If it sounds too good to be true, it probably is."*

I was talking to a friend whose age is same as mine, he has a consulting business. As we were talking he said, "I need to go because my granddaughter is here and I want to play with her." Our dream as baby boomers is to have the financial freedom to live the lifestyle we choose. It means we have a lot left in us and we are not going out to the pasture. We want to work, and not for someone else doing the same thing, but to build a business that allows us to work in our time with the people we want to work with.

The Covey Principle served me well, but I found that I had to update it because the single biggest game changer has been the internet. I had to learn about SEO, meta tags, iframes, squeeze pages, hyperlinks, website development, membership sites, screencasts, and a lot more.

What Can I Do?

Business is simply about solving your customer's problems by delivering the results they want.

I want to discuss some of the problems you might be facing first. When I get asked about starting a business, one of the things that I pick up right away is fear. Inevitably, people are just scared of the things that they've heard or what they believe or what they think is going to happen. So, I want to talk to you about a few of them.

I will be stuck inside my home office -Many think that being a home-based Boomperpreneur means you are going to be by yourself. The reality is you're not. Why? Because you really have to engage with clients, prospects, and friends, you've got to build your network, you've got to be active in your community, so you've got to be out there talking to people. If you will just stay in your house and not talk to anyone, you're really stuck and you are not going to be successful. Being a Boomerpreneur does not mean that you are going to be stuck in a cave.

I don't have what it takes - People believe they don't have the skills to become a Boomerpreneur. They don't have the knowledge, they don't have what it takes. The list goes on and on. Well, you are limiting yourself because I believe you do. You think about all the things that you've done so far in your career that made you successful. These are the skills that you have acquired over the years. It comes down to the knowledge you have, and this is valuable.

Here is the good news: you have faced challenges and tasks in the past. You had to do something you had not done before, but you did. You got it done, you learned how to do this and you got better over time. This means you already know how to do the things that were new to you.

You may need to research or learn something, or maybe you will outsource it, but you will get it done.

I need to develop the next big thing to succeed - The next big thing is right now. Tomorrow is not here yet, yesterday is already gone, but this moment is the time to focus your attention. It is the problem that people are having right now and they are willing to pay for an answer today. All you have to do is focus on what you do well and what you believe is going to be helpful for your client. Don't think of how you will make money first and instead, look to what is needed, what is missing and as a Boomerpreneur, you can fill this void with a service or product you develop.

To answer the question: *I don't know where to start?* You take one small step then another.

Chapter 2

Knowledge Activator Number 1 - Know Yourself

It Starts and Ends With You

If you're a new Boomerpreneur or you've owned and operated a business for a while, you probably have an idea of what success looks like to you. Maybe it's buried deep inside you and only peeks out on rare occasions when you allow yourself to dream, but it is there, and it is important.

If you don't know what success looks like, how will you know when you get there? How do you know what to plan for? How do you know if you're making progress or simply treading water? You don't. So, if your definition of success is buried deep inside you, sit down for a while and pull it out.

- What does it look like?
- How will you know when you're successful?

If you followed my suggestion, you already wrote down what success means to you. Pull it out because I want you to look at it, or if you decided that you would do it later, now is the time to write it down.

Now, be careful. Success can be quickly defined as, "I'm making a million dollars a year." Money goals are just a part of being successful. For some this is not part of the definition at all. If you are 65 or older and just starting your business is that you really want? Or is spending time with your grandchildren more important?

What does your life look like when you're successful?

Are you traveling around the country?

Are you sitting at home in your beautifully appointed home office working quietly?

Do you live by the ocean, in the city or perhaps in the mountains?

Do you work 40 hours a week, or are you a fan of the 4 hour work week that Tim Ferris wrote about?

What are you doing?

Are you writing?
Are you planning?
Are you on the phone talking to people?
Are you giving workshops?
Are you creating?
What are you doing when you're successful?
How do you spend both your work time and your free time?

I want you to do the following exercise, it may be the single most important thing you will do to define what you want, and how you will really know what success means to you.

Find a spot where you will not be disturbed. Relax and close your eyes, begin to see what your ideal day looks like. Make it big and in color, like sitting at theater watching a movie. See yourself in your ideal day.

- Where are you?
- What are you doing?
- Who are you with?

See yourself go through your day.

- What are you working on?
- What kind of car are you driving?
- Is your house paid?
- What kind of business do you have?
- Who do you work with?

Now think about what else you might be doing.

- Are you traveling?
- Where are you going?
- Who is with you?

Write down everything you saw, heard and felt in your success journal, the more detailed the better. Finally, assuming you're able to write out everything that you see when you visualize success, identify your monetary goals. Note that monetary goals are important, however they're not the only aspects of success.

1. Look at what you have written down and circle the words that pop out at you.
2. Do not judge or think about it just let your pen or pencil do the work.
3. Next, transfer these words onto another piece of paper.
4. Do the same thing one more time, circle the words that just jump out of you without judgment… just do it!
5. Transfer these words onto a new piece of paper.
6. I want you to add the words that can turn what you have written down into a sentence.
7. Now transfer this to a 3x5 index card, and add this to your screensaver.
8. This is your "Success Mantra" it is the essence of what success means for you. Look at it every day and keep it where you can see it. Life is tough, we all have our good and bad days and this success mantra can help keep you grounded.

Understanding Change

I want to talk about change. Why? Because you are about to make a change in your life, either to start your business or you want to make a change to take it to the next level if you already have a business.

IBM recently did a study on change. McKinsey also conducted a similar survey, and the number one reason why change initiatives fail is because they failed to change the mindsets and behaviors of the employees and of management.

Think about it: everything we do in business has to do with change. We meet not to discuss problems, but to discuss change. We ask our customers to change from what they're doing to buy our product or service. We ask our team to increase our productivity, to change what they're doing now, to do something different. On a personal note, my wife is always telling me I need to change. The truth is we do have to change if we want to have better relationships and so it goes.

Now, I was taught by one of my mentors many years ago that I could never take someone to a place I myself had not been before. If you're not willing to change, it becomes difficult to expect others to do it themselves. That makes sense. People have antennas and they can sense this, especially when someone says, "I want you to do this, but I'm not willing to do it myself."

You will learn how to change in key areas of your life, to help you improve your relationships with other people, and how to go about getting your goals accomplished, but first, we need to establish a baseline so we have a way to monitor our progress. I want to use a metaphor of taking your car to a mechanic. Before the mechanic starts to work on your car, they need to run a diagnostic. Why? Because they need to determine where the problem is, and what can be improved.

You may have heard of SWOT, which stands for strength, weakness, opportunity and threat. This is often used in business, but we're going to do something a little different here and we're going to use this as a personal SWOT, along the lines of the JOHARI window. It is important to have your journal ready because I'm going to ask you questions, and I'm going to need you to be able to write these answers down.

We're going to look at each area as if we were going through four-panes in a window frame. We are going to begin with writing down strengths. Think of this as the window that is open and everyone sees you, including yourself.

Strengths - List all the things you do well, all the skills, tasks or behaviors you and other people recognize in you. This is the time to brag about yourself. Stop now and write down those strengths.

Weakness - Next, write down your weaknesses. This is the window that you see and others see as well.

List the things or areas that you know you would like to improve. This might be a new skill, or perhaps, this is the skill that would make you much stronger, or sometimes this is the area that your boss or your friends or your peers have said they would like for you to improve. Many times it might be you know you're not as effective a communicator as you might like to be, or you get angry easily. Whatever the reasons might be, take this opportunity and write them down.

Opportunity - The next pane, on the lower left, is the window that if we could take one of the weaknesses, the ones we just identified, and turn into strength.

What would this do for you? What would be different? Take a look at what you have written down as a weakness and just circle 2 or 3 of them that jump right off the page at you. Write down: if you turned this weakness into a success what would be the difference?

Blindside - Alright, we're down to the very last one, this is on the lower right side and is the last pane on the window. This is going to be the hardest one. It is also the one that is going to provide you with the greatest reward. See, this is the part of yourself, your blindside, we deny, you really do not want to look at it but, you know it trips us up.

I will give you an example. My hobby is racing cars — I am an amateur race car driver. In a race, there are anywhere from 30 to 60 cars, all with different horse powers, shapes, sizes and colors.

In one of these amateur races, there was a group of cars called Radicals. Now these Radicals are extremely fast, specially prepared race cars. They are very low to the ground, and did I tell you they are incredibly fast? My car is low to the ground, but these cars are even lower. In the drivers meeting we were told to keep an eye out for them. We were told when you look in your mirrors, you are going to see these cars behind you. You might be thinking there is no possibility they can catch up to you, but they will.

The race begins and I can see the radicals in my mirrors and as advertised, they were fast. As I was coming to a turn, all of a sudden, I can feel that I've been hit on the right hand side of my car. I said "What the hec?" and turned to look out of the window on the passenger's side. All I could see was the very top of a helmet.

I didn't see him. Neither one of us got hurt, but it sure shook me up. My car was banged up, and when I came back into the paddock after the race, I asked my son what happened. He asked "Didn't you see him?" I told him he had come up on my *"Blind Side."* I went out the next day and bought a little concave mirror and put it on my dashboard. People come up to me and ask what is that mirror? "I call it my blind side mirror."

It took me getting hit before I did something about it.

This is the moral to my story: We all have a blind side and sometimes it takes getting hit emotionally before we notice it. The problem is, most of the times we do nothing about it and we just keep getting hit.

I want to share something a little deeper with you. I was working at this company, and our chief financial officer, usually a really nice guy, every once in a while he would call me and he would say things which frankly just pissed me off. I really got to understand about this blindside window. I would get really angry and upset. Did this get in my way? You bet. I would get into a rotten mood. Did this upset the people who were close to me? You bet.

I found out what my blindside was; I was really hearing my stepfather's voice, believe it or not. My stepfather's voice was saying, you're not good enough, you're a failure. I know this may sounds strange to you, but have you ever said, "Don't talk to me in that tone of voice." What does this mean? It was the volume and the pitch of his voice. It would push my hot buttons.

Figure out your blind side and once you know what it is, you do not need a blindside mirror anymore. When it is in front of you this makes it easy to recognize it and not allow it to win over you.

Congratulations! You now have a baseline. This is your gauge for you to measure what you do well, what you need to do, what can happen if you work on a weakness and turn it into a strength, and the most important of all, knowing what your blindside is and putting it in front of you so you can see it.

The Comfort Zone

The risk we run in building and sustaining our business is getting caught in the comfort zone. We are going to learn about the comfort zone, what it is and how to have a breakthrough.

You know the comfort zone is where we get very complacent or comfortable of what and how we're doing in our professional and personal life. We know that we're capable of more, but this would take an effort to go beyond. It's either we don't attempt surpassing it or we just give up.

I'm going to share with you what I've found in my research of what highly successful people do that makes them the best in whatever they do in their career or life. What they have done is they have learned the shortcuts. Now, that's it. This means that they were willing to take a risk and fail at something to learn a better way. These people were willing to stretch; they would try things that did not work and they tried things that worked, and that is how they got better. So what stops us from doing the same thing?

I found out that what really stops us is fear, and this is not just a fear of failing, but it's the fear of success. It's the fear of looking like a failure to your peers.

Did you know that Walt Disney was fired early in his career, and he was told he lacked imagination and he did not have any good ideas? Or that Michael Jordan, the basketball great, said he failed over and over again, which is why he was successful, or Oprah who was told that she was unfit for TV?

Despite the setbacks in their lives, they did not give up. Walt Disney didn't give up, Michael Jordan didn't give up, and Oprah didn't give up. Highly successful people who are not well known, but maybe well known to you, didn't give up.

I shared with you that I'm into racing cars. I had decided I wanted to pursue a life-long desire to race, so I went to a three-day race school at Road Atlanta in Georgia to learn. After completing my training, I rented their race car for seven different weekends to get some practice. I figured I was now ready to race, but my coach told me before I spent the money to have my own race car built, I should first rent a car, participate in a race, and then decide. As it turned out the school offered a race event where you could rent one of their cars and compete in a race series. I was ready to take the next big step of coming out of my comfort zone. I signed up for my first race.

I knew I was ready for my first place trophy in my first race. They would take pictures and I would get a kiss from a trophy girl. I told myself that since this was my first race and everyone else had been racing for 15 years or longer, maybe, I'll come in second or even third, I was determined to be part of Top 5. Now folks, I'm not kidding. What an ego!

I got to the track ready to compete, and I was nervous. My biggest fear I had was wrecking the car so, you can guess what I'm going to tell you next, right? I wrecked. I got into a big spin and ran into the wall at over a hundred miles per hour. Why? Because my ego was bigger than my experience. I learned very quickly on that day what it meant to be humble, and realized that it was going to take more than one race to get the experience.

Here is the worst part. I did not wreck in the actual race. I wrecked in practice the day before the race.

Let me tell you what happened next. The ambulance picked me up, the paramedics checked me out and I was fine, but the car was not. I totaled it. The person in charge of the race, who knew me, said "You know myself and the rest of the instructors were all surprised that you wrecked." I said, "Me, too!" Then, he asked me if I knew what happened and I told him, yes, and explained what I did wrong.

Then he asked me something I wasn't prepared for. "Do you want another car?" In my mind I was screaming *holy crap, no way!* I admit it. I was scared, I was very embarrassed, I had failed in front of all those people and the other drivers. But I knew I was facing my moment of truth: stay in my comfort zone and say "no thanks," or come out of my comfort zone and take a risk.

Just then the mechanic that was assigned to my car said "Rich, we can always fix the car, but we can't fix you, so I'm glad you are alright." I said, "I was okay but I had totaled the car." He replied: "That's all part of racing. If you are not taking a few risks, then you are not racing, and you just learned NOT what to do in that turn." He was right. I said yes to another car.

I had my race car built and competed in a number of races. Four years later my fastest lap time ever was at Road Atlanta where I had wrecked. I had gotten more experience by having a few more spins along the way, but also learned how to control the car. In fact, I have the track record for my class at Barber Motorsport Park here in Birmingham, Alabama.

Getting out of the comfort zone can be scary but highly rewarding. Remember, if you try to take a giant leap like I did, you might be running into a wall. Hopefully, not the same kind as I did. It takes time, with small steps, but the key is not to get stuck with the fear of failing and learn from each setback and become better.

What Do You Believe?

When I'm asked "What is the key to building a business?" I will often answer "It is our beliefs." It is our beliefs about ourselves, our clients, our service, our products, why we are in business in the first place and the list goes on. I have seen businesses fail and succeed because of the power of beliefs.

I define beliefs this way: *beliefs enable or disable my actions.* Actions are movements, they are the process of doing something. Our beliefs can cause something to happen or nothing to happen. Every day, when I put my glasses on, I view the world with my beliefs. My beliefs are made up of my experiences, teachings, environment, and my upbringing, and this drives how I behave and how I judge you should behave.

I was working for a company based in India and I travelled there just about every other month. I would visit the countryside and cities, it was absolutely fascinating to see camels, cows and elephants just walking on the streets with a mixture of cars, trucks, motorcycles and all sorts of other vehicles and people.

I saw some elephants outside the city; the elephant keepers in India have an interesting way of keeping them from running away. They tie them to a wooden peg with a rope. Now, this doesn't make any sense, since a rope like that has no hope of holding the grown elephant… but ask any elephant keeper and he will smile and explain that when the baby elephant is born, they tie its leg to a peg with a rope. At that point, the rope is strong enough to hold the elephant, and the baby elephant quickly learns that trying to escape the rope can't be done. He keeps that lesson within him even as he grows up.

This is great example of a limiting belief. The elephant kept the lesson of not being able to break away from the rope when it was young, even though as an adult it could easily break away, but doesn't.

We often have beliefs that might be useful at first, but then hold us back later in life, long after the original reasons are gone. I want to explain this by using Santa Claus as an example, but I hope I won't upset you by letting you know that Santa Claus is not real. Now, when we were children, we believed in Santa Claus and this belief served us well. We told everyone after Christmas what Santa had brought us. If we were to do this now, as a full grown adult, it would probably get us a one-way-ticket to the closest hospital. You see, all of us changed this belief, replacing it with a new one about the spirit of Christmas, the Spirit of Santa Claus.

Do you remember how much we valued our belief about Santa and the struggles we had learning our new belief? We are not like the elephant. We can break the rope of a limiting belief anytime we choose. Remember, when you heard the word Santa Claus and you immediately have a strong reaction that was associated with it. You would see pictures in your mind. You would hear the sounds of Ho! Ho! Ho! and have all those strong feelings.

I had a limiting belief, which was I couldn't write a book. I decided I was going to change this limiting belief and to do this I needed training on how to write a book. I took action and went to a workshop on how to write a book and self publish it. I met a man at the workshop, who told me the reason he wanted to write his book is because he had been told by a 7th grade teacher "he could never write a book because of his poor writing skills."

He held on to this limiting belief for years until he decided that "I'm going to write a book," and then he told me that he was going to dedicate his book to her, go back to the school and present it to her, just to show her that "yes I can write."

Here is another example. I have a friend and one time, I went over to his house. His wife greeted me and asked me to come in. I asked where my friend was, she said "Well, he's in the living room playing the piano." and I replied: "Really? I never knew that he could play." I walked into the room where he was playing, and it was beautiful. When he turned around and saw me standing there, he got all red-faced. I complemented him on his playing and he said "Well, you know, I never play the piano in front of people because my piano teacher had told me that I could never learn how to play the piano well and I held on to that."

In these two examples, did the teachers mean for their students to take on these limiting beliefs? Of course not. We can take what we hear from someone in authority, family members, friends or even strangers with something they say and take it on as our truth. Once an event happens, then we decide to change this limiting belief and take on a new, more powerful belief that produces a better outcome.

We all have these limiting beliefs. What I want you to do, is just like the rope and the adult elephant, except we're going to easily break it. I want you to bring out your success journal and write down a limiting belief. You might refer to your baseline. Do you remember when you completed your personal SWOT? You might find something there from when we talked about weakness, and what would happen if it became your strength. It might be that the block is a limiting belief.

Step 1 - Think about a limiting belief.

Step 2 - Write it down and think about where this belief came from. I want you to write down how it once helped or benefited you.

Step 3 - Now, write down what's no longer true about it.

Step 4 - Write down what positive new belief you want.

Step 5 - Now write down what you get from this new belief.

Step 6 - Be specific with this new belief, what would you get as a result?

You know for me, I was able to say *YES I CAN WRITE BOOKS*. Whatever it is for you, go ahead and do that now. This is an incredibly useful tool for you to have. Remember, a belief enables or disables an action. It will give you the power to get what you want, when you eliminate a limiting belief.

Goal Getting not Goal Setting

Having goals is a trait of highly successful people and as Boomerpreneurs, we all know this. This is one of the reasons you have this book, achieving a goal of building your business.

I developed the GOAL program not as a way of setting goals, but to accomplish goals. Let's get started in developing your goal getting!

We begin with G of the GOAL program:

Step 1 - Take out your success journal and keep your eye on your watch. For the next 3-5 minutes — do not go beyond this — write down all the goals that you can come up with. Just let the pen or pencil do the work. Just let it flow out, on down to your journal. We have plenty of time to review them later, but right now I just want you to focus on writing them down. Go ahead and do that now.

Take a look at your list when you're done, and I bet you have financial goals and you probably have some towards a better career or building your business, and maybe there's something in there about relationships. Certainly, I would imagine you have some for health, perhaps self-improvement and maybe some spiritual goals.

You know we could spend more time, but I have found that you wouldn't be adding a whole lot more. I really believe it's all been sitting right there, and when given the opportunity to list them quickly, you list the vast majority of your goals, if not all of them. I usually find that the general categories we use are: financial, career, relationship, health, self-improvement and spiritual. What I want you to do next is sort your goals in categories like the ones I just went over.

Step 2 - On a new page of your success journal, I want you to transfer your goals into these categories. On the top of each page write down a category, like financial. Transfer the goals that are finance-related, then repeat the process with each category until you are done.

Okay, so, at this point, you should have listed your goals, and categorized them.

Step 3 - Next, I would like you to circle one, two or three of the goals in each of your categories, but no more than that. Just those that jump out as the most important to you.

Step 4 - I want you to transfer all the circled goals from each category onto a new page in your success journal.

Step 5 - Look at your list and decide which of these are the most important. I want you to circle only the top 3 for right now.

Step 6 - The next step is to place a number 1 next to the most important, then numbers 2 and 3.

Awesome! Congratulations! You are among the few that have their goals written down. You listed your goals, you have category and you prioritized the list. You just completed the G of the goal program.

Outcome

O is outcome.

Step 1 - Go to a new page in your success journal and write down the goal you marked as number 1.

Step 2 - Write down the answer to this question: *What do I really want?*

This is probably the most overlooked question, if you were to just write down a goal without even understanding what it is you really want from it.

Sometimes, because of the language we use, your goal may need to be rewritten. Let me give you an example. Let's say the goal is losing weight. After writing down what I really want, maybe the goal should be to be healthy and live a long life. So, in this case, what is the real goal — to lose weight or to be healthy and live a long life? I want you to look at both of these goals. Which of the two feels more descriptive, more powerful? Which one would you want? I really want to be healthy and live a long life, and a way to do this is lose weight. Does this make sense?

Step 3 - Is your goal achievable?

Make sure your goal is realistic. If we could just pick: *I'm going to be the next basketball player like Michael Jordan*, and I'm 40 years old, overweight and 5'7", then chances are this is not going to happen. Perhaps I could modify it by saying I will be the best basketball player in the over 40 league. Answer this question: Is it achievable? If it's not, then adjust it.

Step 4 - How will I know when I achieved my goal?

I was working with a client I was coaching and one of his goals was to retire early. I gave him a dollar bill and told him to have a great retirement. He looked at me, stunned, and said: "You know Rich, it is going to take more than a dollar." I asked how much he would need, and he didn't know. I said: "Well then! Have a happy retirement."

You get the point; if you don't have a way of measuring it, how are you going to know when you achieve it?

Step 5 - Is this goal under my control?

I have asked clients if the goal is under their control. Sometimes I'll get this answer: "Well, all I need is to have my boss give me that promotion," or "I need my client to sign that contract for the big sale." These types of goals are not under your control, not when you put the responsibility on someone else.

When you are dependent on someone else doing something for you to achieve your goal, you are setting yourself up for a potential failure. This allows you to not be accountable for your own actions. You are making someone else accountable, and with this setup: *I could have accomplished my goal "if only..."*

Make sure your goal is not dependent on someone else doing something for it. How can you make it under your control? What you can do? Okay, you get it.

Step 6 - What resources do I need to get this goal accomplished?

Remember my client who wanted to retire early? I asked him about the resources he needed to get his goal accomplished. He said he needed some education. I asked him to write down the kind of educational resources he could get. He wrote down: *get a book, get a CD, listen to a podcast.* I asked what other resources he would need to meet his goals? "I could hire a financial planner," he replied.

This is your next step: identify the resources you need to get your goal accomplished.

Step 7 - What resources do you already have?

This is often overlooked. You already have knowledge, and you have a network. List everything you have in the way of information, experience and resources that you will use to get your goal done. Make sure you know who you can contact in your network, and who can help you as well.

Step 8 - What are the small steps you can take today?

Most of us make the mistake of having a goal like being debt free. This is good, but it will not be accomplished if all we do is just "set a goal."

It takes going through each of these steps to clearly identify what you want, how you will know when you achieve it, and making sure it is achievable and in your control. Identify the resources you need and the resources you already have. The final step and most important is this... What small steps or tasks can you take TODAY... to get your goal accomplished?

You will be "getting your goals done" if you take one to three small steps every day. Once you accomplish this, take a few more small steps, and soon you will have your goal done, and then you can proceed to the next goal.

Achievement

Now, it's time to work on the A, which is achievement, and how we will work on the steps to get our goal accomplished. A goal without a plan is just a wish.

Take a look at the page in your success journal where you transferred your goals. Go over the list and place the month and year you would like to get them accomplished.

Okay, if you are like most people, then you have way too many goals that you have to accomplish this year. So, as much as you really want to get them done quickly — and I get that — the reality is you need to revisit the list and pick just one that we're going to work on. You can always come back to list to get to the next one later.

Now with this goal, we need to break it down to smaller, manageable parts. Let me explain why this is important. Look at these letters XIBMMTVSATPHDX and study them for a second. I am going to ask you to be able to recall them, then write them down.

I want you to look at these letters and see if you can recall them, ok? Now, write them down. Do you believe that you can get the letters down in the same sequence? Well, maybe you got a few, but it's difficult right?

Now this time, we're going to break it down into smaller parts and see how well you do. This is how we're going to break down the series of letters: X IBM MTV SAT PHD X. Look at them again: X IBM MTV SAT PHD X. One more time: X IBM MTV SAT PHD X.

Write it down and see how well you did. I bet you either got them all, or you got most of them. This is what happens when we break things down to smaller parts, as opposed to one big one.

We're going to use the same approach to break down a goal into smaller steps. This way you can accomplish them.

What you really want to do is to take a page in your success journal, and just answer these questions.

1. What needs to be done?
2. When to do it and in what logical sequence?
3. What will get done by when?

I use *Tom's Planner* from tomsplanner.com to keep track of my projects. It is a simple project planner using a Gantt chart. It is free and is *awesome*. I highly recommend it.

Learning

We've gone over the 'G' where you wrote down your goals, and the 'O' where we discover the outcome, and we just finished 'A' where we figure out how to achieve those goals. Now it's time for 'L,' which is the lifetime learning. A trait of the most highly successful people is that they are all lifelong learners.

Dan Kennedy, a master marketer, was speaking at an event and tells this story about meeting Donald Trump, who was also speaking at the same event.

After few minutes of chatting, he asked Dan: "What three books are you reading right now?" Not, *one* book but *three* books. Why? He wanted to know if there issomething he should be paying attention to in business.

So, let me ask you: "What three books are you reading?" I turn my car into a rolling university. Get CDs from the master teachers and continue to learn. Always be learning and you'll always be succeeding.

Summary

In this chapter we looked at change — what it means to change ourselves. We developed our baseline and even discovered our blindside. Next, we went on to the comfort zone and found out that fear is the cause of staying stuck, and what it takes to break through. Beliefs enable or disable our actions. We found a way to change our limiting beliefs to new beliefs. Finally, we wrapped with learning how not to just set goals, but how to get them done.

You now have the information you need from Knowledge Activator number 1, *Know Yourself*, and it is up to you to take action.

Chapter 3

Knowledge Activator Number 2 - Know Your Message

Many years ago, Charles Kuralt, a journalist for CBS, had a segment called "On the Road." He had an RV, and he and his crew would travel across America, stop in a little town, go into a phone booth, and open up the phone book, randomly picking someone's name. He would then go to their home and introduce himself, and film the segment interviewing this person.

The people he picked randomly were not famous, not celebrities, not reality TV stars. They were just everyday people like you and I. The amazing thing is, everyone he interviewed had an incredible and very interesting story to tell. This was his point. We *all* have a great story to share about ourselves, and so do you.

You Are An Expert

Even if do not believe it... yet.

Take, for example, Jean Nidetch, who was a homemaker in Queens, New York and was overweight. She wore a size 44 dress and was frustrated at all the diets she tried and failed. She had taken a class in losing weight, and it was beginning to work, but her nemesis was cookies and they were calling to her. Instead of listening to their call, she picked up the phone and called her overweight friends. She told them to come over to her house to support her, and each other, in her living room. This was the birth of Weight Watchers.

In Columbus, Ohio there was a small publication called *Columbus Neighbors* that gave actual customer reviews of people who provided home repairs and lawn care. Later it became known as *Angie's List.* Today, Angie Hicks' net worth is estimated to be $50 million dollars.

When I developed my registered and trademarked sales system, it was not because I started out to do this. I was in operations and I took over the sales group. I was surprised to learn that there were no standards or procedures that the sales team followed. I decided to get sales training for the team. When I researched the training programs that were available at the time, I found they were outdated, and missed what the sales people did. Many of them did not even talk about the internet. I decided to create my own system, not because I planned to make this into a business, but out of necessity.

It was only after years of using this system I developed — even using it when I was leading a global sales and marketing team — that I decided to trademark it. Then, I started my business, conducted workshops, and wrote my book.

Remember the first 2 Covey Principles and Keys?

Principle number 1 - Starting a second career in your 50s can be done successfully.

The Key: Believe in yourself and take the risk.

Covey said "The seven principles in the 7 Habits are not original thoughts" - he does not claim to have originated the ideas, but simply to have found a framework and a language for articulating the timeless principles into the seven habits.

Principle number 2 - Take your knowledge and passion, and turn them into a format that can be used and applied to better someone's career, health, relationships, finances or life purpose.

The Key: Create a framework and turn this into a system.

What can we learn from the Covey Principles? He admitted that what he did was not unique, that it was the framework he developed to explain the 7 principles. Notice each of these businesses is not an original idea, but the *framework* is:

- Weight Watchers is a support group and is not an original idea. The *framework* of Weight Watchers is.
- Giving recommendations of local repair services or lawn services is not an original idea. The *framework* for *Angie's List* is.
- Sales training is not an original idea. The *framework* of consultative selling from the perspective of the way your customer wants to buy, not the way you like to sell, from my book is.

What else do they have in common?

- They had knowledge and passion about the subject.
- They turned their knowledge into a profitable product.

- They took a risk in launching and running a business.
- The believed in themselves.
- They all have a message.

Each of these entrepreneurs discovered that within themselves, they wanted to help their targeted customers. How did this happen? They first discovered something that helped them to solve a problem. Then it was their realization that maybe a business could be built to give others what they had found true for themselves. For instance:

- *To be healthier with Weight Watchers.*
- *To help make better financial decisions with actual customer reviews with Angie's List.*
- *To improve career, relationships and life purpose with* The 7 Habits of Highly Effective People.

Research each of these entrepreneurs and you will find how they answered these questions. These are the same questions you will need to answer for yourself as we begin to discover your message.

Your Story

I want you to imagine Charles Kuralt has rolled up in his RV in your town. He is there because he has randomly picked you to interview. He shows up at your house, knocks on your door, and you welcome him in.

I bet you are probably thinking:

- What are you two going to talk about?
- Why would he want to interview me?
- I don't have an interesting story!

You would not be alone. Think of everyone he interviewed, and by the way, he traveled to every state as part of his segments, they were probably thinking what you and I would.

Really, you want to interview me? *Why?*

What if he interviewed a professor from BYU named Stephen Covey, who had just started his business? Or a housewife from Queens, New York who found she was losing weight by having her friends show up in her living room to support one another? I bet we would find their stories interesting. Think about this, how many people do you personally know that have a story that is inspiring, interesting or informative? Perhaps, this person is you.

Before we get started on the next exercise, you might want to consider using mind mapping software. If you do a search on the internet you will find it for free. It allows you to express your thoughts and ideas in an easy way by building a key thought, and then adding branches. In the following chapters and as you build your business, you will find yourself going back and using the mind map many times. I highly recommend it.

Okay, it is time to get your success journal out to because I want to write down your answers to these questions as if you were being interviewed.

- What are the significant events in your life that made you the person you are now?
- What are the achievements you are most proud of?
- What do you like to do for fun?
- What do you like to do in your career?
- How would you describe yourself?
- What would you like to attract in your life?
- What was your biggest fear and how did you overcome it?
- What are you passionate about?
- What job did you have that was most in line with your passion?
- What were the parts of this job you liked?
- What do you daydream about doing?
- Describe someone, alive or dead, whom you greatly admire.
- What are the traits in those you admire most that you yourself have?
- What do find yourself doing that you enjoy so much, you lose track of time?
- What do people come to you ask about the most?
- What do people tell you that they like you for?
- What has been your secret desire to do or be?

- If a genie appeared and could grant you a wish to achieve a goal, knowing you could not fail, what would it be?
- What could you teach someone to do to improve their life?
- How would you like to change the world?
- If there was a slogan or a caption underneath a photograph of you describing your life, what would it say?

Go to your baseline and add your strengths to this list, and ask yourself what could I teach someone? How does this match up to your answers to these questions from above? Are you beginning to see a pattern emerge?

I Need Your Help

What would you tell someone who did the same thing as you for a job, and asked you to be their mentor or guide? Write down your answers in your success journal

1. What do I need to do to be successful?
2. What skills do I need to have?
3. What do I need to know?
4. What could you teach me to be successful?

Having gotten to this point, you should be thinking of the kind of problems you can solve based on your experiences, passion and knowledge. Based on how you responded to the above, write down a clear and concise statement in your success journal by filling in the blanks:

What I know is______ and I can teach ________ to______________ .

Creating your Message

By now you've learned how people began their business, not by creating some new thing, but by taking a problem they were having and figuring out a way to solve it. After time, they all discovered that at some point, there was a potential business. Then they developed a framework, a process, a system and a product. To create your message it first begins with the formula I found that most highly successful people use, no matter their business or their job title:

P+R=S - Problem plus Result equals Solution.

What is the point of offering a solution when you do not know what the problem is, or the result they want? Here is an example from when I did the research for my book, and what I find today when I consult or lead workshops for a client — 90% of highly effective sales professionals follow the model of trying to sell a solution without ever understanding what the problem is.

Here is an example of what happened to me today: I received a phone call and I answered it. The person on the other side said: "Hello, is this Richard Grehalva?" I said yes. He asked "How would like to make more money in your business for just a dollar a day?" to which I replied: "Really, this is your best pitch? Is this the best you got? Give me another line." He began to laugh and he said this was the best he had. I told him send me an email and I would send him a copy of my book.

What is my point? This was one of the worst opening lines I have heard, since he assumed the following:

His message was the most important thing at that moment in time for me... it wasn't.

He thought by telling me the solution first I would melt like butter and want to buy... I didn't.

He figured that if he did the math right, meaning if he just kept increasing his calls, he would make more money... he would not.

He is not the only one who makes this mistake. Entrepreneurs do it as well. This is what they tell me when I interview them, when I ask about their proposed product or service or if they already have one: "My solution is the best." Then I ask the question that gets a response like a deer frozen in the headlights: "What problem does your product or service solve?" Here is how they respond:

It improves productivity. Really, so "improving productivity" is the problem. Isn't this the result they want?

It will make them more money. Really, so "making more money" is a problem. Isn't this the result they want? You get the idea. They never really talk about the problem. If this is the case, how do you get to the problem then?

Pull out your success journal and follow these steps:

Step 1 - Write down the answer to "what problem do you solve?"

Okay, now you probably have written down your answer like my examples above. No problem. We all do this. Yes, even me. It is tough to get to the problem, but now here is what I want you to do.

Step 2 - What problem does (fill in the blank with what you wrote) solve?

Let me give you example: *What problem do you solve?* How to lose weight. *What problem does losing weight solve?* It solves how to stick to a diet.

Step 3 - Keep repeating this process until you get to the core problem.

What problem does sticking to a diet solve? It solves learning to eat healthy and live longer.

Step 4 - This is an example of how this question might be answered:

The problem I solve is... How to eat healthy to live longer.

Now that you can see how this works. Go ahead and complete your "Problem Statement."

Next we are going to work on the result.

I have an example I experienced.

Who can argue that business conditions and new trends are moving at high speed? I want to remain current by reading the new business books that are released. This is a great barometer for me to understand the industry climate. Sometimes, I can't keep up and it just gets overwhelming.

I have a problem, and then I saw this headline on a website and it immediately caught my eye: *So many business books so little time.* It was like they were reading my mind. How did they know this was my problem? They are right. I don't have the time to read all the books I already have, and I'm falling behind. Then I clicked onto the next page, and here is the headline: *Read Less, Learn More* — that was the exact result I was after.

Step 5 - Here is the way to get to the result, and it is real simple: what is the opposite of the problem as you defined it?

Let's look at the problem we just worked on; how to eat healthy and live longer... result: lose weight easily.

Angie's List - Get a customer review of home repairs and lawn care providers to know who to trust to get the work done... result: not get ripped off. Write down what you get as a result when you solve the problem.

We have written down our (P) problem and the (R) result. Now all we need is the (S) solution.

Let me go back to the example where I found a website that looked like they read my mind about the problem I was having (*So many business books so little time*) and they had the result I was after (*Read Less, Learn More*). There is the P+R, now on to the S.

What was their solution? They deliver executive book summaries in a modality where I can hear it, see it, or read it to remain current with the best business books.

The executive book summaries are in mp3, CD and print formats. The summaries are in mobile so I can use my smartphone, iPad, or iPod to listen to the abstracts wherever I am. Each of these summaries provides the essence of the book. From all of the key points, I get exactly what I need and I'm learning more than I was before. Do I still read books? Yes, but these summaries keep me current.

Step 6 - Let me take you through a process to help you figure this out. I call it "Solution Gap." In your success journal go to a blank page. On the left side, write down the problem. On the right side, write down the result you get. In the middle is the gap. Write down... how you can provide a solution for each problem that will deliver the result.

Step 7 - Write out your P+R=S. For example:

Problem: how do you know who to call to get household repairs done from people you can trust? Result: avoid getting ripped off and get good work done. Solution: get reviews from people like you that give honest recommendations.

Now write out yours.

The Message

We are at "The Big Why," and it is time to answer these questions:

Why are you doing this?
Why does it matter?
Why will sharing what you know make a difference in someone's life?

Do you need a mission statement?

I really like what Guy Kawasaki says in *The Art of the Start.* He suggests that instead of a mission statement, develop your mantra. If you are not familiar with what a mantra is, this is the definition:

"A sacred verbal formula repeated in prayer, meditation, or incantation, such as an invocation of a god, a magic spell, or a syllable or portion of scripture containing mystical potentialities."

Just think of the power that comes from a mantra... your mantra.

I decided to help baby boomers to be "Boomerpreneurs." It started with my friend who was 55 coming to me and asking for my help. Then other baby boomers began showing up with the same questions. Through meditation, it was not long before the answer to my own question "what's next?" became very clear.

What I didn't tell you was about my father Greywolf, and the teachings he had or his beliefs. The stories I heard from the old ones began to take hold. Here is one of the teachings:

The knowledge I have is not mine to keep.

The people that I met along the road of life were put in front of me at that time to teach me something I needed to know.

They gave their gifts to me and I must give my gifts away because they are not mine to keep.

What is my mantra? It is simple. "Teaching the Elderly to be Elders."

What's yours?

Your Message

We have finally arrived at the moment to define your message. It combines everything you have done so far. You will be asked "What do you want to do?" This is how you will answer this question. All you need to do is to fill in the blanks.

I teach or show______ to or how ________ how_________even if______________ .

Here is my message:

I teach **Boomerpreneurs** how **to turn their knowledge** into **profitable products** even **if they don't know where to start, or how to get to the next level if they already have a business.**

Chapter 4

Knowledge Activator Number 3 - Know your Market

When I talk about the market, I want us to be thinking of people sitting in a stadium. We are all there because we want the same outcome; we have the same goals and beliefs. We are sitting next to people, instead of thinking of the market as an industry or a job title. We are people helping like minded people. I found out that when I changed this faceless thing to a real person, it makes a huge difference. My approach is putting together my products or services with these people in my mind.

The thing I do, and want you to consider is to have your mantra and message in front of you at all times. I have mine on a 3x5 card taped to my computer screen. I want to be sure that as I develop my products and services, it is in line with my mantra, my message and my customer.

For example:

When I was writing this book, I wasn't thinking of writing it for the masses, instead I thought of Frank and Alicia, both of whom are baby boomers.

Frank is the friend I introduced you to earlier. He wanted to start his coaching business, but did not know where to start. This is why he came to meet with me. He wanted to know how to write a book, build a site and market himself. When I started to put the outline of this book together, I asked myself, what would Frank want to know? What information could I include in this book to give him what he needed to get started building his business?

I also thought of Alicia, a Boomerpreneur who called me after she met me at a conference where I was speaking about tuning knowledge into information products. Alicia's consulting business was stuck. She found her marketing was no different than her competitors. She wanted to do something that would put her ahead and attract more clients. I asked myself what I could include to help Alicia. What could I write about in this book to help her to separate her from the competition, and gain an increase in clients?

Do you notice how this can make the production of your own products and service much easier? Once you make it about real people it changes your mindset.

What is Your Customers Name?

There is power in having a real customer's face to refer to as you develop your products and services. This is called *creating a persona*, which is usually a fictional person, to understand their needs, motivations, demographics and environment; to understand the buyer. I like to use real people instead of fictional ones as this makes it easier and much more real for me. I recommend you do the same. At the end of the day, putting on a face you know will help you identify with them and by doing this you can serve them better.

When I'm buying presents for someone in my family it is easy to visualize them. I can think about what they might want and enjoy based on their needs, wants, desires and motivation. This is why I want you to use the same approach. I want you to think of your customers in the same way. What are their wants, needs and desires in terms of content, services and products?

For example, when I buy a present for my wife who is 63, versus my youngest son who is 26, versus my grandson who is 10, one present will not fit all. It is based on their age, their interests, married or not, where they live and what their hobbies are. The same things you want to know about your customer. What blogs do you read? Where do you go online for information to help your business or career? What social sites are your favorites? These are the same questions you want answers for about your customers. This helps you to understand how better to promote your product or services.

Now it is time for you to identify your best or ideal customer. Make it someone real, and write as if it were an interview. Better yet, call the real people who are your personas.

Here are questions you might ask:

- Name?
- What is your age?
- What is your relationship status?
- What country, state and city do you live in?
- What is your occupation?
- Tell me a little about your background.
- What are your goals?
- What is the current problems you are facing?

- What is creating these problems?
- What online blogs, sites, and social pages do you go to?
- What offline publications do you read?
- What online and offline events do you attend?
- When you are learning do you like to read a report, listen to the information or watch a video?
- What is dream and how could I help you?

Okay now you have your own Frank and Alicia. Think of whoever it is for you as we continue on to the rest of these chapters.

What is Marketing, Anyway?

Peter Drucker, an icon in management and business said this: "Because the purpose of business is to create a customer, the business enterprise has two — and only two — basic functions: marketing and innovation. Marketing and innovation produce results; all the rest are costs. Marketing is the distinguishing, unique function of the business."

Here are the definitions I use to describe this:

Marketing - "The Right Product" at "The Right Price" to the "The Right Person" at "The Right Time"

Innovation - The ability to see what is NOT there and then create a product or service to fill this gap.

It is time to look at The Covey Principle again. Remember, he admitted what he did was not unique; it was the framework he developed to explain the 7 principles. Notice each of these businesses is not an original idea but the framework is.

Weight Watchers is a support group and is not an original idea. The framework of Weight Watchers is.

Giving recommendations of local repair services or lawn services is not an original idea. The framework for Angie's List is.

Sales training is not an original idea. The framework of consultative selling from the perspective of the way your customer wants to buy, not the way you like to sell, from my book is.

I want you to think about the framework differently. Look at what each one did with an "Innovation" viewpoint: the ability to see what is NOT there and then create a product or service to fill this gap.

There were plenty of diet books and services, but what was missing? A support group of like minded people.

When Steve Jobs introduced the iPod, what was missing? A mobile storage device that could hold thousands of songs.

There are lots of books for entrepreneurs, but what was missing? A book to help baby boomers turn their knowledge into profitable products.

Take your P+R=S statement and view it from the "Innovation" mindset. What is missing that you could provide, or is it already there?

Use what you did in "Solution Gap" to look at the problem you solve, and the results you provide with this new perspective about the solution. What products or services can you offer that fills this void of what is missing? Take your time. This is a very important step. Do not over think it. It is really about simplicity; making it complicated by overthinking does not make it better.

Here ideas are some great ideas to help you. Go to Amazon and look at the best-selling books on your topic. Read the reviews people post, both good and bad, what they liked and disliked, and what they wanted addressed. *Hint:* this may be an opportunity to create what is missing.

If you have downloaded your mind mapping software, this is an ideal time to use it. I want you to brainstorm on this. I know you want an answer now, but take your time. Let it sit for a few days and then go back and review it. Make any changes that make sense to you.

Next, I want you to test what you have done by asking your customers — I mean the ones that you built to be your personas. I also want you to ask a few people you trust that are in your network, and who could be potential clients. I want to tell you that this could be difficult. After all, this is where your passion is. I want you to listen to them. Do not judge their comments. Take their feedback as information and motivation. Make any suggested changes, and go back again for feedback. Once you get the information, you can confirm that you are the right path. Congratulations!

Summary

You've identified "The Right Person," and "The Right Solution." You've done a great job by developing your message, defining the problem you'll solve and developing a solution, defining the results your customer is looking for and discovering what is missing in the market, and identifying a product or service that will fill the gap.

In the next chapter we will begin to build your product.

Chapter 5

Knowledge Activator Number 4 - Know your Business

"I hate to sell." "I don't like to sell." "I feel uncomfortable selling."

This is just some of what I have heard from my clients. How about you? Do any of these resonate with you? If not great, but if selling makes you uncomfortable, I have good news for you... Don't sell and you will be successful.

Let me explain by reminding you of what I shared with you in an earlier chapter.

I want to remain current by reading the new business books that are released. This is a great barometer for me to understand the industry climate. Sometimes, I can't keep up and it just gets overwhelming.

Right Person - I had a problem. This is where it starts, because no sales person told me I had a problem. I knew I had a problem. Next, I saw this headline on a website and it immediately caught my eye: *So many business books so little time.* It was like they were reading my mind. How did they know this was my problem? They are right; I don't have the time to read all the books I already have, and I'm falling behind.

Right Person - I was drawn to the website page because the headline listed my problem. I then clicked through to the next page, and where the headline was: *Read Less, Learn More*, and that was the exact result I was after.

Right Time - I did not need anyone trying to sell to me. The headline was strong enough to confirm what I wanted. What was their "Solution?" They deliver executive book summaries in a modality where I can hear it, see it or read it to remain current with the best in business books.

Right Product - The solution saved me time and gave me what I needed. The Executive book summaries are available in mp3, CD and print formats. The summaries are mobile, so I can use my smartphone, iPad, or iPod to listen to the abstracts wherever I am. Each of these summaries provides the essence of the book; from all of the key points, I get exactly what I need and I'm learning more than I was before. Do I still read books? Yes, but these summaries keep me current.

Right Price - The product is offered in different formats and different price points.

I want to explain what just happened with this example. I was looking to go from my current state, where I was today. The problem was time. I wanted to get to a future state, where I wanted to be; feeling informed, current and satisfied. I was looking for the transformation to get from point A to B, which was a summary of the books I want to read in a format allowing me to listen to the key points on my mobile devices... when I had time.

The place between my current problem or state, to the future state where I want to be, is called the "Transformation." This is what our customers and clients are after, and this is where you and I come in.

You bought my book not because I sold it to you. You wanted to get from point A to point B, and the information in my book is helping you through this transformation. I do this by providing results to the problem you have, with possible solutions.

This is the new belief I want you to take on, and let go of the limiting belief about selling. If you have this limiting belief, then go back to the chapter *Know Yourself* and follow the process of eliminating limiting beliefs, and the steps to get the new belief.

What Is My Business?

1. Our job is helping people through the transformation of where they are now, to where they want to be.
2. We do this by providing services and products, eliminating their problem, and getting the results they want.
3. In exchange for our client receiving our knowledge contained in our products and services, we receive money.

This is it! It is not complicated so long as you follow these 3 steps.

I want to spend a little time going over the information in step 2 — "We do this by providing services and products, eliminating their problem, and getting the results they want" — because this is the first time I'm introducing you to some new information about P+R=S with a new formula.

What Is Value?

In tons of marketing material or sales talk, salespeople will say they provide "value." Okay, sounds great, but what is it? And how do you measure it? When I was doing the research for my book *Unleashing the Power Of Consultative Selling,* I asked customers and clients these two exact questions.

I created this formula based on what they told me: R-P=V which stands for *Result Minus Problem Equals Value.* When the product or service "Eliminates my PROBLEM and I get the RESULTS I was after, then this is how I measure VALUE."

Who can disagree with this?

Think about the products and services you have bought. If they eliminated the problem and you received the results you wanted, you are satisfied and will tell others. If they didn't, and you are not happy about your purchase, you will tell other people not to buy it.

This is why I wanted to spend time addressing step 2 — "We do this by providing services and products, eliminating their problem, and getting the results they want." It is a simple statement but if we fail to deliver this... we will fail in our business.

Value Continuity Circle™

After I published my book on consultative selling, I began to look at the impact the internet has made on selling. In fact, I no longer even see the title of salesperson as being the correct title in today's connected world in the age of the consumer. There is a term I'm sure you have heard, the "Sales Funnel." It is taught and talked about as what is needed in all types of sales and marketing training, in books and products on and offline. What I began to question is: Is the sales funnel as we know it still as relevant today as it was when it was first adopted?

The sales funnel was introduced in 1903. No, this is not a typographical error; it really was introduced over 100 years ago.

A quick overview of the sales funnel is:

- We load the top with suspects.
- Suspects go through a qualifying process.
- Prospects continue to be qualified.
- The best prospects are worked.
- They are identified as a potential sale.
- They are signed and become a customer.

There is something else that was introduced around the same time as the sales funnel, a slot machine. It works on the same principle — put money in the top and hope for a jackpot to come out in the bottom.

I asked myself this question: *"What is missing?"* Then I thought what if we turned the sales funnel upside down, and instead of a slot machine, it became a vending machine?

The picture I had in my mind was that of an hour glass. Why an hourglass? It looks like two funnels to me. The top one is pouring the sand through a focused opening filling in the bottom half. This is the image I had as I developed the framework for my new system I call *The Value Continuity Circle*™. Here is how my *Value Continuity Circle*™ works:

The Moment-of-Truth - It begins when we know we have a problem. The "moment-of-truth" is when it has gotten to the point that it is bad enough to do something about it, or we decide we want to get a goal accomplished.

Search - Over 80% of us go online to search for products or services that can solve our problem.

Content - When we find a product or service website, we are looking for content: videos, testimonials, and information that helps us with finding a solution to our problems. This is finding suspects in the sales funnel.

Social Conversation - We go to social sites and forums to get comments from people who have used these products or services before, or recommendations of vendors or companies they have used successfully. This is turning a suspect into a prospect in the sales funnel.

Decide - We have searched on the internet, reviewed the content, looked for what other people had to say and have now narrowed the list to a few prospects from which you will pick one vendor or company to do business with. This called qualifying the prospect to the best few in the sales funnel.

You see the sales funnel is still being used, but not by sales managers or small business owners. It is now being used by the consumer. It is the top part of the hourglass that looks like a funnel with the sand pouring, filling up the bottom half. This is means the old model of searching for suspects and prospects is happening all the time, but it is being done by your potential customers every day. What is coming out of the hourglass or top funnel is you; your product or service may have been identified by your potential customer as a qualified prospect.

Here is an example: An event planner was putting on a conference and the topic was consultative selling. He went on the internet to look for potential speakers and went through every one of the steps I mentioned above. I received an email that said he wanted to hire me to speak on this date for a certain amount of money. Was I available? I had never talked to him or submitted a proposal. He was not *my* suspect or prospect but I was *his*. I spoke to him and agreed to speak at his event. There were over 450 attendees and I sold out of my books.

What I'm telling you is that this really happens and it leads to new customers or clients!

Okay, now let's look at the bottom half of the hourglass as I describe in the *Value Continuity Circle*™. These are the steps my client took when he found my website and then asked me to speak at his event. This is what you must deliver on your website to meet your customers' expectations.

Certify - Your website must quickly confirm that you:
- Understand their problem.
- Can deliver the results they want.
- Provide a solution that eliminates their problems and gives them the results they want.
- Offer a product that is unique and valuable because it fills the gap of what is missing.

Content - When you visit websites, what are you looking for? Are you looking for someone trying to sell to you, or good content that can help you with your problem?

Do you want to see instructional videos, free reports, and blogs with tips that can help you? Or videos of guys with a Ferrari in front of their mansion, showing you receipts of how they make 6 and 7 figures, while telling you how you can be making thousands of dollars overnight, just by buying their stuff and working just one hour a day? The internet was not developed for free marketing; it was developed for content. TV is dependant and depended on for advertising.

To confirm you are a potential prospect for your perspective customer or client, you must provide them with great content in a modality they prefer. They may want to read reports, white papers, and books, or watch videos and read testimonials to get a feeling about you.

Systematic Questioning - We have 2 motivations: "To avoid having a problem," and "To move towards a goal or objective." What went through your mind as you selected this book? What has been going through your mind as you have been reading my book so far?

Have you been noticing as you read these chapters that this information will help you "avoid the problem of how to get your business started?" or has it been giving you the information "moving you closer to accomplishing your goal of starting your own business?" One of these statements has meaning, the other one not so much. There is no right or wrong answer. It is just how in this situation the direction motivates us. Our language becomes very important. Depending which question I asked, you would get a response or you would ignore it.

Presentation - This is where your product or service is presented to your customer. It can be an eBook, instruction or how-to videos, DVDs, CDs, mp3s, seminars, or speaking.

Validation - Once your customer validates that their "moment-of-truth," their reason for seeking a solution to their problem, can be satisfied by you, your product or service, they will buy again.

What is the continuity circle? Once they have bought a product from you, you must continue to build your relationship by providing great content. It is not talking about what you have to sell, but giving them information that will help them. Letting them know about a product you have after providing content is a powerful way of building a trusting relationship.

Creating your Product Map

If you have come this far in the book, then I hope you have done the exercises. You have a success journal with your answers to the questions I have asked you. You have done some mind maps. It will make developing your product map easier. If, otherwise, you have not, no worries. You can do this as we develop the product map.

Before we get started it is important to have this mindset. I want you to change your mindset about creating your product map for yourself to a mindset of building a product map for one of your personas. In my case, I'm building Frank and Alicia's product map. After all, they are the ones that will be buying my products and services, not me.

The place we start is by asking this question: "What is the problem my customers or clients want solved right now?" And then create a product or service to solve it. If you do this, then it will make it much easier to create "The Right Products" at "The Right Time." If you build products and services you think they need based on what you believe, it can lead to a whole lot of work that nobody buys. Trust me, I've made this mistake.

I use a process in my business called 'Compression Planning," developed by my friend Jerry McNellis. I use it for my VIP Days, one on one coaching, all types of consulting engagements and even used it to create the outline of this book.

It combines storyboarding with accelerated facilitation techniques to eliminate meetings that just produce more meetings. Compression Planning generates results, and I have been using this process for 20 years because it works! The reason I share this with you is it also uses prototyping, based on techniques used by Leonardo da Vinci. Instead of investing the time and money on a project, he would first build a prototype.

A small, working model should be made first. It is much easier to find out what works and what does not work by doing this. Did the idea meet the purpose it was designed for? Changes could be developed and retested and a decision to go forward or not is based on the results. This is what you must do before making an investment of time and money in building your services and products:

- Survcy your clients and customers
- Develop a list of questions and send a survey out to your list asking "what are the biggest problems they are having right now?" The questions need to be sent to the people you identified in your niche.
- Go to Amazon and see what books are best sellers in your niche and read the reviews to find out what people want.
- Go the blogs and forums where your clients or customers go. Read what they are talking about.
- If you have some ideas on products or service then send out a survey. Ask the questions "Would a product or service that addresses (problem) with (product) be useful?" Ask more questions and promise them something for filling out the survey. Offer a free report or eBook in exchange for providing you with this valuable information.

What We Need for the Product Map

The model we are going to follow is, you guessed it "The Covey Principle," as outlined earlier.

P+R= S Statement - You will need to have your problem plus result equals a solution statement. This gives you what type of products that you can develop.

Personas - This is who you are building the products for. Have all the information you collected during the interview questions you have answers to their wants, needs, desires, goals and dreams.

Success Journal - Hopefully, you have been maintaining a success journal where you have been writing down your notes, thoughts and ideas.

Developing the Product Map

Your product map is made up of three things:

1. The product topics that are most likely to be marketable
2. The related products you can build off of those topics
3. The order you want to produce them in

Here is what I mean using "Building a Consulting Business" as an example:

What product topics are most likely to be marketable?

Consulting, for many Boomerpreneurs, is a logical and perfect way to start your business. You have a set of skills that companies and a particular industry or market need, and you can offer your services as an independent contractor or freelancer. I want to you think of your career this way: go back to the beginning years as if you were starting as an apprentice, then move on to your journey and finally, be a master at your craft. It has taken you many years, many mistakes and many successes, to achieve the understanding, the processes in what you do, in a way that delivers the results that individuals are looking for and find valuable.

Now, because you are going to be trading your time for money — in other words, if you're going to bill an hourly rate — there are only so many hours in a day that you can actually bill for. This can be a happy problem if you find that you are running out of hours in a day, and a curse because you no longer have the freedom you were after when you started your business.

What related products can you build off of those topics?

Follow these 5 steps in building your consulting business as the expert in your field; take from the idea of moving through the stages of your profession from apprentice to becoming a master.

1. Answer these questions:
- What are the short cuts?
- What are the steps that most people do not realize?
- What are the steps to be successful that are measurable and achievable?

2. Create and build your services into smaller packages.
- Break down what you do into 5 to 7 smaller chunks. Try not to make it any more than 7, but the absolute maximum is 10.
- Each one of the packages must have:
    - A problem it solves
    - A result it delivers

- A solution with a process to accomplish it
- It must have a start and end, with specific deliverables

3. Determine the hours it takes to accomplish the deliverables. Next, and this is important, figure the value to the potential client.
- Will it save time?
- How much time?
- Will it save money?
- How much money?

4. Determine a price for each package.

Now you can develop your price, one that delivers what your client wants for a fair price with results. This means you price the package based on *value* not on hours. Rule of thumb says your product should provide 10 times in value, so a $97 dollar product should deliver a $1000 dollars of value.

5. Name your system and packages.

People want to understand what you are doing so, I want you to come up with a name for these packages and then a name for this system. Now what do I mean? Edward Deming says *"If you cannot explain what you do as a process then, you don't know what you are doing."*

You see what you have done is created processes in each of these packages and combined this into a system. This approach is solving a client's problem that delivers results for the value they see as fair. This is a win-win situation. Congratulations, you just created the outline for your online product map!

What order you want to produce them in?

This is best done using a mind mapping software. If you have not downloaded it, yet now is the time. At the end of the day this will be the easiest way to brainstorm your ideas. It is easy to review and make changes. We build one map then break it down to smaller specific maps by product.

Take these packages and develop instructional videos, eBook, reports and seminars. Build membership sites, download digital products and physical products.

This will decrease the need to trade hours for dollars once you follow these steps. But guess what, when you do this your consulting gigs will increase because now your prospective clients see you in action and want you to help them. More good news is that you can be selective of which consulting engagements you do because you have a stream of revenue coming in.

The product map for Frank and Alicia is:

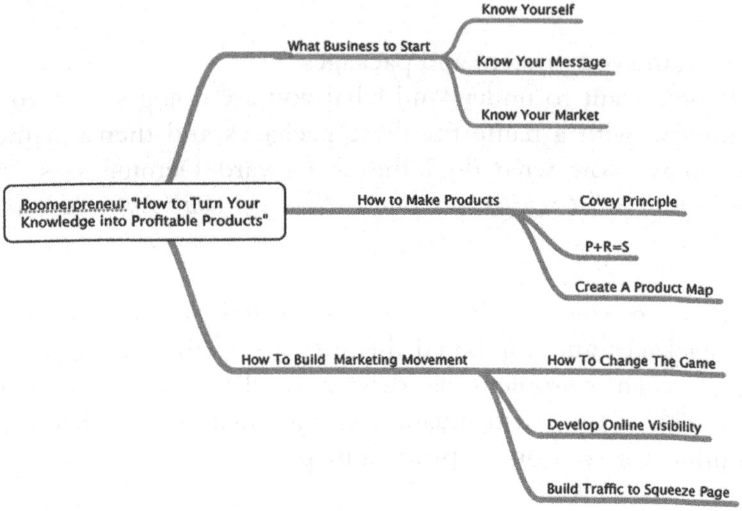

Here is an example of what products I will be developing in sequence.

Go ahead and start to build your product map and the sequence in which you will develop your products.

Chapter 6
Knowledge Activator Number 5 - Know Your Movement

Every small business owner, expert and entrepreneur makes the same mistake. They try to be a smaller version of a big company. A big company will out resource, out market, out finance and out sell you unless you change the game. This is not a criticism. I made the same mistake when I first launched my business and failed. Here was my reality: I had learned what I know about business by being part of big business.

I remember consulting for a small, 10 person company and I asked "Who do you compete against?" They proudly replied IBM. I said "Really, how do you set yourself apart from IBM?" *They didn't.* They had the same marketing approach that was easily forgotten. Their website and marketing was trying to look like IBM, just a smaller version. Their problem was their entire annual marketing budget was what IBM spent in a few hours.

I have a question for you: What if you were the 7th largest brewery and decided you were going to increase your marketing to be number 1, but then you discover their marketing budget greatly surpasses yours? *What do you do?*

You "Change the Game" by coming up with *Tastes Great!...Less Filing!* and with that, Miller Lite took the company to number 2. For a short while Miller Lite had 100% of the light beer market.

I want you to consider the language Miller Lite used in starting a movement — people who wanted and enjoyed beer with less calories and carbohydrates — what did you like? The taste, or that it was less filling versus regular beer? People are very loyal to their brand. To compete effectively and move ahead of your competition means stop doing what they do! If your marketing looks and sounds like them, then how does your customer select you versus them?

Being the low price, high quality, we care about our customers, we provide speedy service and the list goes on of what you do, is the same as your competition. If you compete against a big company and try to be like them you lose. They have access to resources you don't have. How do you change the game? Becoming the expert with ebooks, videos, information products and becoming the site, the place, the person where your movement, your community who look to you as someone who can help them overcome a problem or gain a goal.

This is what this chapter is written to do, to help you become the Go-To person.

At the beginning of this book I said: "You are an Expert...You just Don't Realize it Yet." I have been talking about "The Covey Principle," and using this many times to describe the steps of becoming known as an expert. If you have followed everything in this book up to this point, you should realize your *Knowledge is Valuable*. It is unique; you have uncovered what is missing and can fill this *Gap* with a product or service. If you have NOT come to this understanding about yourself... reread the book.

I'm going on the assumption that you do realize and have come to accept this fact: You do have a *Gift* to give, it is your wisdom and the world needs it. It is time to do what it will takes to *Change the Game* from your competitors. You will become the *Trusted Advisor* in your niche. You will have a following, a community, a movement.

Sharing Your Story?

To be a trusted advisor people must know you and your story. I have had clients say to me "I don't really have anything to teach? How could I create a following?" I then ask them to tell me their story, the story behind the story — the one they don't want to tell me. This what I suggest to them after hearing some of their stories.

What if you wrote a book on:

- How To Be a Good Father
- Confessions from an Addicted Housewife — How I Beat My Addiction
- How To Be Successful Against The Odds
- The Real Story Behind Success and It Isn't Money

These are just a few titles of programs I have suggested to my clients. These are powerful personal stories, and to hear them gives us inspiration and motivation to do better in our lives. Why? Because if they did it, so can you, if they show you the way. What steps do you need to take, will they help you? I will ask you, what I ask them.

- Do you think that people would want to follow you?
- Do you think there are people who want to join this movement?
- Do you think there are people who want to know what you know?
- Do you think there are people who want to get past the same obstacles?
- Do you think there are people who want to achieve the same goals?

I'll bet you are saying "*Yes.*"

To create a relationship with the people in your movement, be honest and tell them something about yourself so they can relate to you. Stories are powerful, stories are how we learn. I know for myself, when I was younger, I just wanted to rub up against the Grandfathers; I was hoping some of what they had would rub off on me. I learned from the stories they told. Now, I pass the stories on to the next generation. You have a story to tell the people in your community, the people who want to join in your movement.

Look at the story of Star Wars. Luke is our hero, who has a wise mentor in Obi-Wan Kenobi; this first wise old man gives him guidance. Later, he meets another mentor, Yoda. He does battle against evil and the dark side in the forms of Darth Vader and the Emperor.

Read mythologist Joseph Campbell's book *The Hero's Journey,* to really understand the power of story.

I want to share with you my 5 Principles of Change. To understand the basis for the 5 principles, I need to share a little bit about myself. This comes out of my story, from what I learned from my teachers. It comes from going through many changes along the way in my own life. I know firsthand how difficult change is, but the reward is well-worth it.

You see, my success was predestined before I was even born; what I could achieve was decided before I took my first breath of life.

Let me explain. I grew up in East Los Angeles, a very tough neighborhood where even the poor told my dad, Greywolf, we were poor. So, I left high school in my senior year to help support the family but, I got married at eighteen, was a father of two wonderful kids before I was 21. My mother died of a drug overdose when I was 23. And I was divorced when I was 28.

I could have been just one more statistic, but I decided that I was going to change, that I was going to change my mindset, and I was going to be successful. I have to tell you, the road was not easy.

I was told I could never be promoted to vice-president in a Fortune 500 company that I was working for... but I was. I was told that I would never be able to travel and work internationally, but I just spoke at an event... in the 22nd country I've been to. I was told I could never write a book... but I did. I was told I could never start a business... but I have. I was told I would never be able to own a race car and be an amateur race car driver... but I do, and I am.

"I do it because I can, I can because I want to, I want to because you said I couldn't and I knew I could."

When I share this story, as a speaker or as part of my workshops, I always have people come up to me afterwards and thank me. They tell me how it touched them. Often, they share their own, very personal, stories with me. This is the payoff for me. If sharing this somehow helps someone else, then I will continue to share my story over and over.

When the Student is Ready the Teacher will Appear

I've had teachers and mentors who taught me about peak performance techniques, interpersonal skills, motivational processes, business planning, facilitation techniques and much more. The elders taught me ancient wisdom. I learned from my mentor Dr.Ron Hering, from my father Greywolf, and from my adopted Grandfather Selo Black Crow about ritual ceremonies to celebrate a spiritual wakening of the human spirit.

I found through a successful career — being a Vice-President, General Manager and as a Senior Vice President in areas such as global sales marketing, systems immigration, and strategic consulting — that while I had business skills, I knew where my real passion was; combining all that I had been taught, to help others. It was teaching peak performance and mindset change processes with ancient wisdom to help people to live their life purpose.

This is what I have taught for the past 20 years, leading men's intensive personal development retreats and business leadership workshops. I teach business and life success skills because they are not separate parts of who we are. Both parts live inside of us. The problems start when they do not live in balance. These parts end up fighting with each other, until you find someone who can be your guide. This is why my message of *Teaching the Elderly to Become Elders* is needed in these times. Youth is celebrated and the old ones are forgotten. Not anymore, not with you and I leading this *Movement.*

What I just shared is a true story about myself. I talk about areas in my life that are sometimes hard to discuss; where I grew up, my mother dying of a drug overdose, people judging me because of my background and having people who told me I couldn't succeed, all the time knowing I could.

There were many dark days, but many more brighter days. I remarried, and we just celebrated our 30th anniversary. I have a wonderful family, friends and great clients. I embraced the teachings of my father and the Elders. I'm successful according to what is important to me, not by someone else's view.

When I share an authentic part of myself that is real and not staged… people want to follow. They want my help.

Never forget people have very sensitive BS antennas. I have been on the stage with other speakers who cry when they tell their story — at the same place in their talk every time — I swear I think they bite their lip to do it.

Hopefully, you are beginning to understand what a movement is, and what it looks like. It is, at the core, really about a relationship with the people in your movement, in your community. Just be honest and tell something about yourself so people can relate to you... not the image of what you think you should be.

My 5 Principles of Change

Principle Number 1 - Change means — you have to take action immediately.

Now you're saying to yourself, "d'uh," but here's a fact: Two things you need, information and action. Many of us get the information but then don't take action. We're all saying *I want to start* and at the time we really mean it. We say we're going to start tomorrow, next week, next month, but we don't so… why is that?

Most often, we want way too much, too quickly, and there's a part of ourselves that just wants to put on the brakes. Why do we want to make all of these changes? We've been fine with what we've been doing, it has been working for us. Bottom line is, the voice in our head says: "*why change now?*"

So the key here is we want to take one, two, or three small steps, immediately. We don't want to try to take too many things on, too quickly. That never works out, so the key is one, two, or three steps, immediately, today.

Take action.

Principle Number 2 - Change means — you have to change your thinking.

I know you've heard this one before: "*If we keep thinking the same way, we will get the same results,*" and it is so true. We need to change our minds from what we are today, to where we want to go, or be. Get a vision of what that is. Once you have that vision, then you will need to go out and get the training, get the resources, find like-minded people, or get a mentor or coach to begin thinking differently. Ask yourself, what can I do today, to turn my new way of thinking, to help my new vision of myself become real?

Principle Number 3 - Change means - you have to change your environment.

The environment that I'm talking about is the one inside your mind.

What I've done is turned my car into an institution of higher learning, and I do that by listening to educational CDs, I listen to the inspirational words from the masters and elders. I listen to book summaries that give me the essence of what they're saying that might be helpful to me. In my physical environment, I make time for relationships — family, friends, nature, meditation and spirit.

Principle Number 4 - Change means - you have to change your focus.

You know what Steve Jobs did when he returned to Apple? *Focus.* He eliminated 350 products to focus on 10. He removed the clutter that got in the way of what Apple did really well.

We must do the same thing in our lives. We need to eliminate the clutter and the non-important things that we do, and focus on the three to five important areas that will improve our personal and professional effectiveness. The key is to pick the one that brings us the greatest results, just like Steve Jobs did at Apple. Follow his pattern, eliminate what you cannot do, and focus on what you will do to bring you these benefits.

Principle Number 5 - Change takes time.

Stick with it and each day is better than the day before. There are no get rich overnight schemes, there is no push-a-button and everything is magically going to be different from tomorrow cure. It's going to take time, and if anyone tells you otherwise, they're just not telling you the truth.

You know there are going to be setbacks; this is part of the process, so expect them, learn from them, and continue on your path. Self-made millionaires do not succeed on their first try. Statistically, it's something like seventeen before they actually are successful, but they never view the past sixteen times as failing. They just use the information they can get so they don't repeat the same process, and they move forward — just like you will. So, learn from the setbacks and you"ll make progress..

I can tell you firsthand as you take these steps, "This day will be better than yesterday, and tomorrow will be even better, so long as you focus on this moment to take the steps to live your purpose." Do this, and you will have unbelievable new levels of success.

So now you know what I and many others have used to get our successes. Write this down in your success journal. Better yet, write this down on a three by five card or make it a screensaver, and place it on your desk, put it on your mirror, put it on your computer, your tablet, put it wherever you may be able to see it, and refer to it every day.

- I take action.
- I change the way I think.

- I change my environment.
- I change my focus.
- I accept change takes time.

What Do You Need to Create A Marketing Movement?

One part of creating your marketing movement is about developing a community of "like minded" people. Here are the parts:

Unity - We must be connected, for example: "We are all baby boomers."
The Story - I was working, was laid off from my job, and finding a new job was tough. I was not ready to retire, I still wanted to be productive. I wanted to start my own business.
The Challenge - How to become a Boomerpreneur, develop products to pass on our knowledge, and make a difference.
Freedom - Creating financial and lifestyle freedom in retirement for myself, my spouse or partner, and family.
Transformation - "Teaching the Elderly to become Elders" by launching a business.

To show you an example of a marketing movement, I begin with asking you a question: "What is the difference between the latest smartphones from Samsung, Blackberry and Apple?"

It is this: a marketing movement where people stand in line to be one of the first to own the latest Apple product. This is what Apple's competition has not figured out, how they changed the game. You can argue that the other phones may be better, but no one can argue Apple's success in developing their global marketing movement.

Let's apply the 5 parts of creating a marketing movement to Apple:

Unity - We use white earbuds.
The Story - Simplicity in design, and maximizing the user experience.
The Challenge - I'm a PC and I'm a Mac.
Freedom - User intuitive interface.
Transformation - "It just works."

Steve Jobs was legendary in his presentations and product launches. Go to YouTube and watch some of his presentations, study his techniques. I guarantee it is worth your effort to study his presentation style, slides, and words, and how he created excitement for Apple's products.

Creating Online Visibility Websites

"If you build it, they will come," is a line from a movie. In real life, they won't come unless they know about you, what you have to offer, and why they should care.

Let's begin with your website. I want you to go online and go to the IBM website. Click on to the products, services and industries you will find over 85 choices to make.

Overwhelming? You bet.

Now, go to Apple's website, and you will find 5 choices.

Easier? You bet.

What if you build your website and only gave your prospective customer one choice?

Focused? You bet.

Now, having a website with everything you have to offer is important. This will point your prospective or existing customer to a targeted video squeeze page. You need a website, but don't be like IBM with so many choices. Follow the Apple model with fewer choices, but always develop a video squeeze page for each of your products. This is where you start, by building a video squeeze page. Why? Because it is well-focused. It will focus on building your list. It shows your community — the people who will want to join your movement — who you are, and how you can help them.

Step 1 - Build your video squeeze page.
Here is what you need:

Headline - Get your customer's attention by having it contain their problem and result.
Benefits - Show what your visitor gets, and how it will help them to avoid their problem or achieve their goal

Video - Talking about and showing them why you are the onc that can help them.
Call To Action - What's in for me? Your free teaching videos.
Opt-In Form - For customers to sign up, where they fill in their name and email address. You will need to have an autoresponder as well.

Step 2 - You need to 3 videos with great information and educational content.

I'm talking about content so good, you could easily sell it. I bet you're saying: *"If people would buy it, why would I give it away?"* The reason you do this is — how else are your prospective customers going to know if what you have, is what they are after? And how else will they get to know you?

Do this knowing not everyone will take action. The important thing is giving away some information that may help someone, and that is a good thing. The goal you want is for your prospective buyer to say to themselves: "This information is so good, I wonder what else he/she has? It has to be great if this is what you get for free!"

Step 3 - The fourth video is your offer.

This is when you let your prospective customer know what product you have to offer; what they have seen in the previous videos was leading up to this moment. Let them know how they can get the results they are after, and eliminate the problems they have been having. This is why they have taken their time to watch your previous videos. They want what you have to give.

This can be a membership site, an online product, an audio product, DVDs, or a seminar.

Okay that's it. It is not complicated.

Setting Yourself Apart as an Expert

What does it take to be an expert? What did we learn from the Covey Principe? It takes a book.

My regret is waiting so long before I wrote my first book. Don't make the same mistake. I get emails asking what someone should do first. I tell them — *write and publish a book.*

When I'm flying and the person next to me asks what I do, I tell them I'm an author. The response is always "Really? What is your book about?" I ask for a business card, and tell them I'll send them a copy. I *always* get a business card and a potential customer to add to my list. I am an expert in their eyes.

My book is a required text book at a graduate school of management in France, as part of their International Project Management course. eHow.com uses my book to explain consultative selling. I'm the expert in understanding consultative selling, and if it is not me then tell me who is? This is the mindset I want you to begin to take on in your market niche.

There's a saying I read, which says there is a book inside all of us, and many of us want to write it. Our problem is, how do you write a book and get it published? We just don't know how to do it, we just don't know how to get in front of these big publishing houses.

But, you know what, when I first wrote my book, there were a lot of rules like how many pages a book must have, the steps you'd need to take to get your book proposal in front of a publisher, and how to get an agent. The book publishing process is a very strange business, and to explain it well, that's a whole chapter by itself.

So what changed?

The internet changed the game, and changed it in a big way. Anyone can become an author and self-publish. The big publishing houses sell books to major brick and mortar book sellers, while Amazon is selling books — and especially eBooks — to people. And they have something the book publishers do not have: an email address.

Who has the better business model? I will leave that up to you to decide, but I know who I will put my money on.

The number of people that have the ability to read an eBook on one of their mobile devices is really astronomical. We have seen a huge increase in the number of eBooks that have been sold and downloaded through iPads, Nooks, Kindles, smartphones, and even to laptops and computers.

This is a great opportunity for you, especially if you like writing. Don't worry, because even if you don't, I can still give you some ways to figure out how to get a book done. Here's the thing — you can write and publish a kindle book for free, and it can be done in 30 days or less.

Now, I know that sounds impossible, but it *is* possible and it is actually being done. I developed the outline, wrote this book, had it edited, had a cover designed and had it published in less than 30 days. I know since I did it, so can you.

Remember with an eBook, there are no rules. An eBook can be 30 pages, it can be 60, 90, a hundred or more. Just go to Amazon Kindle right now and do some research. Look at the topics that interest you, because you need to have knowledge in that topic, and look at the top sellers.

You know what else you get with the Amazon Kindle publishing platform? You don't have to pay to publish it. Amazon also helps your marketing, and you get a royalty. It does not get any better.

The price for an eBook can range free to 99 cents, to $2.99 and up. You determine the price, but $2.99 seems to be a good price point.

Now can you make money at it? Have you heard of the book *50 Shades of Grey* by E.L. James? It has sold over 65 million copies worldwide. Now with the availability in hardcover, *50 Shades* will complete an almost entirely reversed 'traditional' publishing cycle. The books started out as *Twilight* fan-fiction posted online. A tiny Australian publisher then released them as eBooks and print-on-demand paperbacks, selling about 250,000 copies. Random House snapped up the rights in a seven-figure deal, re-released the ebooks and made *50 Shades of Grey* widely available in paperback for the first time. It achieved incredible success.

I'm not suggesting this will happen for you. What I'm telling you is that eBooks are not only an acceptable format, but people buy them.

The added benefit is that when you write a non-fiction eBook, it helps establish you as an expert. It will do this in whatever business you are choosing; it could be your consulting business, it could be your services business, or any business you are in.

Bear in mind it is necessary, now more than ever, to set yourself apart from your competition — and to do this you need a book. The good news is that it is pretty easy to do. Write your eBook about what you know; do not try to write your first book on something you do not know, or know very little, about.

Here is how I do it:

- Decide on a topic.
- Get a few packs of 3x5 index cards, and write down the questions that you get asked most.
- Sort the cards for the 10 best questions.
- Go to Amazon and look at the reviews of the books on your topic. Review the comments of what people like and pay special attention to the unfavorable reviews of what they did not like, but wanted.
- On your index cards, write down the points. I have found in the reviews people will comment on the points that helped them. Sometimes, they even write it down in the 5 or 10 things they like. The same is true when they write what they did not like.
- Place these cards under the 10 questions you wrote down
- Under each question — which is a chapter heading — begin to list a sub-topic on each card.
- Add up how many sub-topic cards you have, and sort it down to the best 10 to 20 under each question.
- Add 2 more chapter cards; the first is the introduction and the last one is the summary.

An eBook is somewhere from 80 to 100 pages but remember there are no rules here. It can be 50 pages or 500 pages. A page has about 300 words at 12pt font.

- Review the index cards and verify you have 10 sub-topic cards under each question; write 2 to 3 pages per card and you have a 200 page eBook.
- Don't like to write? Then get the Dragon Speaking program, and dictate it or record it, and have it transcribed.
- Then, go on eLance.com and hire an editor to edit your book.
- Go to Fiverr and get an eBook cover made.
- Go to Amazon Kindle (KDP) and follow the instructions to have your eBook published.
- Create a landing page to promote your book.
- Send out an email to your list, Facebook, etc.

- Amazon helps your marketing through Amazon Select and when you create an author page.

It doesn't get any better. Get your book written and published. You can begin to build some revenues and identify yourself as an expert. CongratulationsI on becoming a published author!

Why You Need Videos

The number of unique users visiting YouTube every month has reached 1 billion; "*Nearly one out of every two people on the Internet visits YouTube*". This is why you need and must have videos, enough said.

There are only three things you need to create a basic video product:

1. *Your audio/video recording hardware.* I use a microphone/headset for doing screencasts, and I use the video camera on my iPhone or iPad, and a Kodak Zi8 camera (cost $100 on Amazon). I use a remote microphone because this is very important. People will not forgive bad sound on a video recording.

2. *Your video editing software.* This is the program you're going to use to open up your 'raw' recording, and refine it a bit, doing things like trimming out parts you don't want, and making it sound better. There are quite a few options available to you. I use Screenflow because I use a Mac. If you have a PC then Camtasia is your best bet. The learning curve is very short, and for both products and you get a 30 day free trial. If you want tutorials, all you need to do is go on to YouTube and you will find them.

3. *Your delivery system.* This may be via YouTube, or it may be private, where it is on your blog or website only.

These are the three things you need to get your videos and video products out the door. Record your video, edit (if necessary) and convert it, and deliver it. You can make it simple, or, if you have the time and want to do it, you can add really slick features.

So let's talk about how to record your video. There are two basic types of video you can create for your products, screen captures or 'talking head' videos. One is not better than the other — there are times when each is a better fit for what you're delivering — but each requires a different kind of setup.

Again, you can make both of these video types complicated, but we're going to talk about the very simplest way to get going, so you can ship your videos, solve customers' problems and make some money.

Let's talk about how to get your first videos done by looking at the two types of videos you can make.

Screen Capture Videos - These are great for tutorials and presentations.

The simplest way to get a video out is by doing screen capture, and is ideal for doing presentations if you are using PowerPoint or Keynote. With screen capture videos, you don't have to worry about what you look like, or what the lighting is like, or how well your video camera/webcam works. You can just get going and deliver good content, and if you have to edit it by clipping things out here and there, it is easier than 'talking head' videos.

All you need for this is some screen capture software, and a USB microphone with a headset, or you can use a desktop microphone for better results.

Talking Head Videos - This is a great way to connect to your community.

People, when they get to see you, begin to create a bond that is much stronger than reading a blog or an article. For them to see you in even a short video will make a difference in how they relate to you. The good news for you is that it's easy and very affordable. I bought lights, backdrop, video camera and software for under $600. I do not recommend using the webcam on your computer to do any of these type videos. Using the video camera on your smartphone with tripod attachments are very inexpensive. No backdrop or lights? No problem — go outdoors; early morning or late afternoon lighting is best. There is no excuse, and it is easy to do.

Let's talk about these in more detail.

Do I need a script?

Imagine you have been asked to speak to an audience of people that you have been trying to get in front of for a long time. The audience is made up of your ideal customers, and the promoter tells you there will be 500 attendees. AWESOME! And the topic is in your sweet spot.

Then the promoter says, "We want to video your talk and promote it online so thousands of people can view it." The date is a few weeks away. Do you say...no problem? Will you show up and wing it, or do you prepare an outline for your talk? Will you rehearse your talk? Will you figure out what to say when you get on stage, or do you review what you've written down?

You get the point. Some people can and do just wing it. I can do this, and sometimes it works, depending on the situation.

Here is what happens with a video. You have 1 to 2 minutes to get your point across, and have a high retention with your viewing audience. Many people recommend 30 seconds, but a longer video of 8 to 10 minutes works for how-to or educational videos. The best audience retention I have on my videos is 2 minutes or less, the longest is a little over 4 minutes.

I recommend using a script. We can speak at about 140 words a minute, so a 3 minute video is 420 words. A page is about 300 words so try for 280 words or less. Write your script, then go back and edit out the words you do not need. After you do this, go back and edit it again. I usually write my script and edit it once on one day then, I go back the next day and edit it again. This is what works for me.

Do you a need a teleprompter? You don't have to have one but it helps. I have an app I downloaded and use. I also have a music stand that I have right underneath my video camera, and I have my script on my laptop with a remote. I don't read my script word per word, I will add some different words or reflections to make it feel a little more spontaneous. I have found that this keeps me on track and my message is much better that to just start talking for short videos. For some videos I just have an outline of the 3 to 4 key points I want to make, practice it a few times, and then shoot the video.

I have found that it is usually the second or third take of the video that will be the one I use.

I don't want to be on video - Get over it.

Are you one of those people who do not want their photo taken because you are afraid the camera will steal your spirit? Of course not. This is a limiting belief. If you plan to speak, run seminars or meet with customers face-to-face, they are going to see you and hear you. So, what's the difference?

Remember you can always do screencasts if you still do not want to be on video.

Speaking to Your Community

I'm not going to spend much time on this topic because you already know if you don't communicate to your customers, clients and community, they will go somewhere else. Here are a few more things you must have to keep your community engaged:

- Blog
- YouTube Channel
- Facebook page
- Twitter
- LinkedIn
- Articles
- Teleseminars
- Webinars

These all serve as ways to link people to your websites. The more you can get your message out through the social sites and other online places, the more it becomes necessary. Winston Churchill said *"We make a living by what we get. We make a life by what we give."* This is why building your movement and your community with products through which you share your knowledge is needed.

I wish you all the best as you become part of the Boomerpreneur Revolution.

Chapter 7
One More Thing

In *The Power of Intention* by Dr. Wayne Dyer, he writes on the 7 faces of intention. One of the faces of intention is love. He says, "If you aren't doing what you love and loving what you do, your power of intention is weakened...You attract into your life more of the dissatisfaction that isn't the face of love." Consequently when you are doing what you love, what you're passionate about, you attract more into your life.

Passion also brings excitement and motivation when your strengths and passion are aligned. Now is a good time to look at what you have written down in your baseline, your personal SWOT. It was one the very first exercises I asked you to do.

When you know what your strengths are and when you know your blindside too, it gives you the power, courage, and information to make wise decisions about your business and your life. Look at it, keep it close, otherwise your blindside can creep out and bite you.

Along the same lines is our beliefs about money, and the rules we set for ourselves. We create financial habits based on rules we've learned from others, and then develop our beliefs. These rules may be exactly what you need to do to achieve financial abundance, or they may be your limiting beliefs that will get in your way. I'm not going to judge or tell you what my rules and beliefs are. I'm not going to tell you that yours are right or wrong. I just want to encourage you to explore your own beliefs and rules.

Some rules of wealth may be:

- Save 10% of every paycheck
- Live within your means
- Give 10% to charity annually
- Spend 20% of your profits on marketing

I trust that you will make a wise choice. The one thought I have always had in my mind is *do the right thing by treating others the way I want to be treated.*

You now have increased your responsibility beyond your immediate family. Once you follow what I outlined for you in this book, it means you have added a community of people who share the same goals and challenges. This is why they are in this movement. You owe to them to do what I will share with you as my final thought:

"The gifts that we have been given by those who were placed in front of us on the path of our life, was not an accident, these gifts are not ours to keep... we must give them away."

I wish you much success in your business and life.

Richard Grehalva
Birmingham, Alabama
April 2013

About Richard Grehalva International Inc.

Richard Grehalva — *"The Grey Hair Entrepreneur"* — is a recognized industry expert on persuasion and influence for creating mindset performance strategies in consultative selling, leadership and life.

Richard is the founder of the Boomerpreneur Product Blueprint, where he teaches small business owners, experts, and Boomerpreneurs "How to turn their knowledge into profits by becoming the trusted advisor in their market, even if they do not know where to start or already have a business."

As an author, trainer and motivational speaker, he has had an impact on people and organizations worldwide. Richard also successfully developed a trademarked sales methodology called *Sales Mapping: The Process of Connecting the Dots and Winning Customers for Life*™

He transformed an exceptional background in senior executive leadership roles in companies throughout the world (over 20 countries) into leadership consulting for operations, sales, marketing, business development, project management and change management.

He is a Master Practitioner NLP, a Certified Trainer for Accelerated Behavior Change, is trained in the Language and Behavior Profile, is a member of the Experts Industry Association and is a Compression Planning facilitator.

Richard also incorporates the teaching philosophy of his father Greywolf, a Native American elder and teacher, into his programs. To maintain his competitive spirit, he is an award winning racecar driver and sometimes includes his live video feeds from the track to illustrate his points in motivational speaking programs.

You can visit his website at www.RichardGrehalva.com.

richGREHALVA INTERNATIONALinc
Business and Life Success Skills

Additional Resources

For additional resources and information on Richard's live event please go to: www.TheGreyHairEntrepreneur.com

For information on learning how to build your online business please go to: www.BoomerprenurProductBlueprint.com

For information on 2VIP Days one-on-one coaching go to: www.ResultsNotAdvice.com

For information on Richard's trademarked sales methodology, outlined in the book *Unleashing the Power of Consultative Selling*, visit: www.ConsultativeSellingBook.com

Richard has produced a FREE eCourse with 21 videos on the questions he gets asked most often about consultative selling. To get immediate access to these free tips go to: www.TheConsultativeMindset.com.

Made in the USA
Monee, IL
04 November 2026

67375823R00056